LUNCHBOX

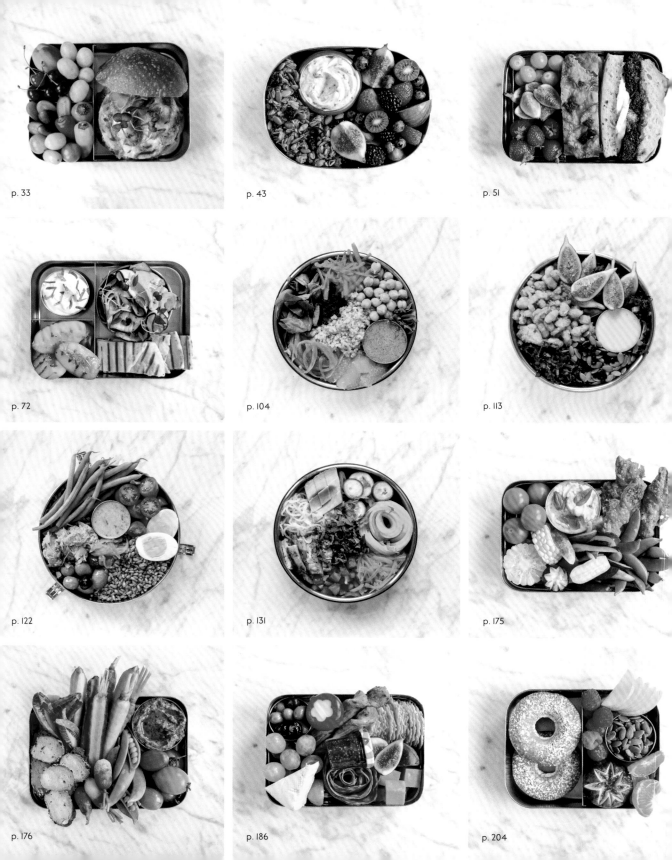

LUNCHBOX

75+ Easy and Delicious Recipes
for Lunches On the Go

AVIVA WITTENBERG

appetite

Appetite by Random House® and colophon are registered trademarks of Penguin Random House LLC.

Library and Archives Canada Cataloguing in Publication is available upon request.
ISBN: 978-0-525-61152-3
eBook ISBN: 978-0-525-61153-0

Photography by Aviva Wittenberg
Cover and book design by Emma Dolan
Printed and bound in China

Published in Canada by Appetite by Random House®,
a division of Penguin Random House Canada Limited.

www.penguinrandomhouse.ca

10 9 8 7 6 5 4 3 2 1

appetite   Penguin
by RANDOM HOUSE   Random House
                  Canada

For Evan, Noa, and Talia,
my absolute favorite lunch eaters.

CONTENTS

INTRODUCTION

For every weekday morning of my childhood, I was a clock watcher. Sitting in the classroom, I'd study the minute hand traveling around the clock that hung on the wall, counting down to lunchtime when I could finally tear open the day's brown paper bag and see what my mum had packed for me. (And this was especially the case on Fridays, when I knew there was a special sweet treat in my future.) I'm all grown up now, but little has changed about my love of lunch— I still look forward to digging into whatever has been prepared and taking a moment (and some-times it is just a moment) to hit pause on the day and enjoy a bite to eat. The difference is that now *I'm* the resident lunch packer, and I'm packing lunches every day for my family of four.

I spent years working in an office in a windowless cubicle, then upgraded to more years working near a window with a view of a parking lot. So I know how important taking a proper lunch break can be. I always made the point of slipping out of the office for a quick walk to clear my head, and when back at my desk, I'd kick off the afternoon with some lunch. The lunches I brought from home were always the best ones (rivaled only by the dumplings made daily at the little dim sum place in the food court down the street), and I took great joy in creating that delicious meal for myself.

A few years, and two daughters, later, I joined the daily grind of packing school lunches. At first it was a struggle—I'd gotten used to packing my own lunch, but adding two more was tough— and yet, through trial and error, I fell into a routine that made this daunting task seem not so daunting after all and resulted in lunchboxes returning home empty (well, most of the time!). After a few years of being in the swing of things, I started sharing what I packed for my girls' lunches on Instagram. It came about accidentally, when my daughter desperately wanted her own Instagram account to stay in touch with friends. After some negotiation, we agreed she could have an account if I could follow her—which meant I needed an account too! At the sug-gestion of a friend (who is as food-obsessed as I am), I started sharing what I was making for the girls' lunches most days. I'd always taken pride in the lunches I prepared, and it felt good to share. I quickly found a community of parents, caregivers, and lunch eaters of all types who were looking for lunch ideas and sharing theirs. This book is a collection of all the tips and tricks I have learned along the way, as well as more than 75 of my go-to recipes for lunches on the go.

This book is for anyone who packs lunches, whether they're for yourself or someone else. My goal is to make life easier for you, and lighten the stressful morning time crunch that many of us experience, with delicious lunch ideas that everyone will enjoy. The recipes you'll find inside this book are all simple, straightforward, and, for the most part, speedy: they count on great ingredients, rather than oodles of time, to deliver a big hit of flavor for your midday meal. They reflect what my family enjoys eating on a regular basis, the kids included (and you can read more about my approach to kids and lunches on page 10). They include both old favorites from my childhood and new favorites influenced by the variety of food we've eaten in our hometown of Toronto or discovered in our travels around the world.

You should be able to find everything you need to make these recipes in a regular supermarket, but if I had any doubt, I've noted an alternative that will do the trick. And remember, you're packing *your* lunch here (or your family's lunch) and not my lunch, so make substitutions based on what you have in your fridge or pantry and what works best with how you prefer to eat. These are lunch recipes, after all (not blueprints for building rockets!), so play around, have fun, and make them work for you.

Welcome to the world of great-tasting lunches on the go! Say goodbye to vending-machine sandwiches, pallid pastries, sad desk lunches, and lunchboxes that come home untouched. Open your arms to making your lunch break (whether it is 55 minutes or just 5) a special moment in your and your family's day—one that's worth clock watching for.

Exceptional Egg Salad Sandwich p.48; Hummus p.183; Baked Pear, Vanilla, & Spice Donuts p.204

Weekly Meal Plan

	Mon.	Tues.	Wed.	Thurs.	Friday.
Lunch	Autumn Caprese	Crd. roll-bowl w/ leftover chicken	Quesadillas w/ raw veg	Tom Soup w/ grilled cheese	Buy lunch!!
Dinner	Roast Chicken + veg	DIY rice + bean bowls w/ veg + cheese	Roasted tom. soup + sandwiches		
Snacks	Apple Carrot Muffin		Granola bar w/ fruit	Rice pudding Muffins	

On hand:
2x delicata squash
1 bunch chard
1 bunch kale
3 x sweet peppers
½ red cabbage

tofu
eggs
1x chicken

cheese
cheddar
cream
fresh mozz

LUNCH PACKING STRATEGIES

Lunch packing can be a daunting task. I've had my fair share of Monday mornings staring into a fully stocked fridge, wondering what on earth I am going to pack in the empty lunchboxes lined up on the counter. Over the years, I've developed a certain set of lunch strategies that have proven (time and again) to work for me and my family. They've been successful both in reducing the stress of the morning and in delivering delicious lunches we look forward to all morning long. In addition to what you'll read below, I've also put together five differently themed lunch plans to help inspire you. Find those on pages 215 to 218.

PLAN AHEAD

Set aside some time on a day or two a week to do advance lunch planning. I know it's not an earth-shattering suggestion, but it works! Pick a manageable block of days to plan for—some people like to sit down on a Saturday and plan the whole week ahead, some just the first 3 days, and some the next 3 weeks! Do whatever works best for you. I eased myself into a meal-planning routine when I used to drop off my then 3-year-old daughter at her 45-minute dance class each week. I'd say goodbye and zip down the street to a café, order myself a cappuccino (and probably a cookie!), and loosely map out a week of lunches and dinners in a notebook. Then I use that plan to compile my shopping list. For me, it was—and still is—a simple way to free myself from mealtime decision making all week long, and to remember to try new recipes I've been inspired by (and to come back to old favorites).

START WITH WHAT YOU'VE GOT: I take a blank page in my notebook and start by writing out what we already have in the fridge on the right side of the page. Then I draw a quick grid for lunch and dinner from Monday to Friday, and use the fridge list as an inspiration for filling it in. Flip through this book and pick out the recipes you're going to make, then add the items you don't already have to your shopping list. As well as making for efficient lunch planning and grocery shopping, the bonus of the fridge-first approach means I've really reduced our family's food waste.

BE FLEXIBLE: One caveat: be open to changing your plan when you get to the market! If there are some gorgeous local fruits or vegetables that catch your eye, do not let your plan get in the way of buying them and adjusting your menu.

CONSIDER PERISHABILITY: Delicate leafy greens, fresh herbs, and fresh berries have a limited lifespan, so if you grocery shop on the weekend like I do, start the week with lunches that include the most perishable items first and wrap up the week with hearty greens like kale or chard or with other vegetables or fruits that have a longer shelf life, like carrots, bell peppers, apples, and oranges. I usually plan for fully fresh-food lunches on Monday, Tuesday, and Wednesday, and for something that I pull from the freezer or pantry accompanied by some longer-lasting produce for Thursday and Friday.

MAKE AHEAD

Once you've planned your lunches, give yourself a block of time once or twice a week to make them (or just components of them) in advance, to get ahead of the lunch game. In each recipe in this book, I've called out if all or part of the recipe can be made ahead to help you plan. Some suggestions regularly in my rotation:

Carrot & Orange Soup p.82

PRE-MAKE STAPLES: Sauces, dips, and dressings can be made a few days in advance and stored in the fridge to grab and go when the time comes.

ALWAYS HAVE SOUP ON HAND: Soups last really well in the freezer, usually up to 3 months. Batch-cook soups and then freeze in 1-cup portions to make it even easier to pull them out and defrost when you need them. Or, take a look online for purpose-made silicone trays in different portion sizes—they allow you to freeze soup, stews, etc., in blocks and then transfer the blocks out into freezer bags for long-term storage—they're incredibly handy and a worthwhile investment to make packing soup for lunch a breeze.

BATCH-COOK GRAINS: Go-to options like quinoa and farro can be made in advance and stored in the fridge (or even freezer) so that they are ready to go when you are. If time doesn't permit, you can buy frozen or shelf-stable packets of cooked grains to keep on hand.

ADVANCE-COOK PROTEINS: Grill or roast boneless chicken breasts or thighs (or buy a rotisserie chicken and divide it into portions); marinate and grill some tofu, then cut into "steaks"; sauté some shrimp; or hard-boil and peel some eggs. If you have dry beans in the pantry, cook a pot of them and pop them in the fridge for later in the week.

PREPARE VEGGIES: Peel and cut up carrots, slice cucumbers, chop celery, and store them in containers either submerged in water or with a damp cloth to keep them fresh so that you can pull them out when you're making a salad or need a side with lunch.

BATCH BAKE: Snacks and sweet treats like muffins can be baked ahead and popped into the freezer to set yourself up for the week.

DINNER IS THE NEW LUNCH PREP

Haven't you heard? Dinner is the new lunch prep! This is the strategy that I am most grateful for, especially on hectic mornings with little time to spare. By preparing lunch the night before, mornings become a breeze. To do this, I regularly make what I call DIY dinners, where everyone constructs their own meal! I put all the different ingredient components out on the counter in separate bowls and we get to work building our own bowls with the ingredients we love—and then, by strategically prepping extra food, we then pick and put together our own lunches for the next day, too! I've found DIY dinners are the key to making everyone happy at dinnertime. My family members, like many families, have divergent food preferences. For starters, we have two vegetarians and two very, very enthusiastic carnivores. Some of us love vegetables, some don't. And we have two very strong-minded soup factions living under one roof: puréed versus non-puréed! But a DIY dinner is designed so that everyone can assemble exactly what they like.

TRY DIY DINNERS: At a high level, each DIY meal has some kind of grain or carb base, a choice of protein, a few vegetables, and a sauce—and maybe I'll throw a few fun toppings into the mix, like crunchy or pickled onions (page 178), seeds, nuts, or whatever I can pull out of the pantry. Here are my top five DIY dinners and their packable lunchtime variations:

1. **DINNER**: Soba noodles (or whatever noodles I have) + miso broth + crispy tofu or chicken (see page 139) + steamed veggies
   LUNCH: Noodles topped with tofu or chicken + steamed veggies + an insulated bottle of broth on the side

2. **DINNER**: Rice + black beans and/or sautéed shrimp + corn + sautéed mushrooms + avocado + salsa + pickled onions (page 178) + green onions/fresh herbs (cilantro or parsley)
   LUNCH: Large flour tortilla filled with rice + beans + any selection of the above, then wrapped
   LUNCH: Quesadilla made with a handful of leftover protein + herbs + cheese

3. **DINNER**: Sushi or other short-grain rice + tofu or fish + fresh julienned vegetables + avocado + crumbled nori + pickled ginger + spicy sriracha mayo
   LUNCH: Onigiri—rice balls stuffed with leftover protein, sprinkled with sesame seeds, and served with a slaw of the julienned vegetables

4. **DINNER**: Fresh Roll Bowl (page 131)
   LUNCH: Salad rolls made of leftovers rolled up in rice paper

5. **DINNER**: Meze spread of hummus + baked store-bought falafel + roasted peppers + Vibrant Quinoa Salad (page 104) + roasted sweet potatoes drizzled with tahini + quick green salad (including whatever other vegetables I have in the fridge)

LUNCH: Pita packed with falafel + hummus + leftover salad odds and ends

PLAN FOR LEFTOVERS: If DIY dinners aren't for you, you can still use dinner to your advantage. For example, simply make a little more than you need for dinner so you have leftovers for lunch (like leftover roast chicken to top a salad or grain bowl). Or you can double the recipe you're making for dinner and transform the leftovers into something new (the Warm Bowls (& Handpies) chapter, page 146, has you covered for ideas here). Or if you're already roasting something in the oven? Add a sheet pan of vegetables for tomorrow's salad bowl. Or you're having couscous or quinoa? Add some extra to the pot so it's ready to pack as a grain bowl for lunch the next day.

PREPARED FOOD FOR THE WIN

I use my freezer as a kind of cold pantry and keep it stocked with prepared food items—some homemade and some store-bought—for quick and easy options when I'm most short on time. (Look for the freezer-friendly icon in the recipes for items that you can freeze and pack away for the future.) There's no shame in picking up a tray of sushi, a selection of antipasto, or some samosas, spring rolls, or dumplings at the grocery store. Looking in my fridge/freezer might lead you to believe that I'm set for a cocktail party. But these little nibbles are easy and delicious options when making something from scratch is simply not possible.

THINK OUTSIDE THE (LUNCH) BOX

Remember, lunch doesn't need to be a single large item (although I give you plenty of options for those in this book). An assortment of smaller items can be just as satisfying. Combining a muffin, some yogurt, and fresh fruit; or a dip, flatbread, and sliced vegetables; or some cheese, crackers, dried fruit, and seeds are all fantastic midday meal options.

KID-SPECIFIC STRATEGIES

A quick note on my philosophy about kids, food, and lunch: I firmly believe that good food is good food and that kids can and will eat the same food as adults if exposed to it and not restricted to a limited selection of "kid food." Unlike when I was a child, kids now are exposed to a steady stream of food media and are much more adventurous and open to trying the new things that they see on the screens around them—or see their family and friends eating. There are also excellent food magazines and books to encourage kids to think openly about food and even learn to cook from the time they are toddlers.

INVOLVE YOUR KIDS IN LUNCH PLANNING: My advice is to involve your kids in planning their lunches, give them choices, and better yet, give them this book to mark lunchboxes that appeal to them! Even the most adventurous eaters have preferences (one of my girls will sit down and eat a plate of octopus but will not touch a red pepper!), and it's important to respect those so that they'll eat and enjoy the lunch they take to school and be set up for an afternoon of learning.

CONSIDER HOW THEY'LL EAT LUNCH: Aim to pack lunches that are age/dexterity-appropriate and that consider dining conditions. Cutlery can be fiddly for younger kids and will slow them down, so stick to finger foods like sandwiches and rolls, or get creative with things like pasta threaded onto a lollipop stick for easy eating during their lunch hour. My kids used to have about 20 minutes to eat, which meant that a bowl of salad greens was out of the question, and filling foods that they could eat in a few bites were the way to go.

CONSIDER WHERE THEY'LL EAT LUNCH: Some years, my kids ate their lunches while sitting on the gymnasium floor, and other years, they ate at their desks. We discovered through trial and error (and some minor disasters) that bento boxes with lids that stay attached take up so much space that they are just asking to be tripped over if placed on the floor—launching lunch into the air—so we made the switch to bentos with detachable lids that year!

MAKE IT ACCESSIBLE: Be sure your kids can open up the lunchboxes and containers you send them to school with, and test them out beforehand. Finally, even though one of my daughters is one of the most avid readers I know and dives between the covers of a novel or two a week, she will not open the cover of a container if she doesn't already know what is inside. Bento boxes are perfect for kids like her because she can see everything that is packed for her at a glance, and I use a liquid chalk pen to label the outside of thermoses, insulated drink bottles (with smoothies inside), and other containers she cannot see into.

DON'T BE DISCOURAGED: It's important to keep in mind that kids will invariably bring home a partially or completely untouched lunch at some point—in fact, this will happen more than once! Do not feel defeated and discouraged. Sometimes the call of the playground is so great or a conversation so compelling that lunch just doesn't get eaten. Feeding kids is a long game, and one, two, or ten missed meals will not matter in the long run.

PRESENTATION MATTERS: To keep things fun for younger kids, think of ways to make lunch presentation creative and fun. Things like egg molds that transform hard-boiled eggs into teddy bears and other adorable characters can bring a smile to a little one at lunch. Little plastic food picks are a cute addition to a lunchbox too, and were a great way to make lunch eating fun for my kids when they were little. Pay a visit to a Japanese market to stock up on fun and whimsical lunchbox accessories.

NOTE: *I have left nuts completely out of these recipes so you can be assured that anything you make for your kids will respect the nut-aware policies in place at most schools.*

RECIPE ICONS

Look out for the icons below to guide you to the recipes that are particularly suitable for making ahead of time, and storing in the freezer until you need them, or that come together in 10 minutes or less, or that can be easily adapted to different dietary needs, or that are especially good for certain times of year, or for kids—or all of the above! And turn to page 212 for a handy list of all the recipes in each category.

 MAKE AHEAD & FREEZE

 QUICK & EASY (10 minutes or less)

 VEGETARIAN (or easily adapted to)

 VEGAN (or easily adapted to)

 HOT FOOD FOR COLD WEATHER

 COLD FOOD FOR HOT WEATHER

 GREAT FOR KIDS

LUNCH PACKING GEAR

It won't surprise you that as a champion lunch packer, I have strong opinions on the containers for packing your lunch on the go. I learned through trial and error that while investing in good-quality lunch gear is costly up front, it can last a lifetime. I've spent more money on replacing poor-quality lunchboxes that have broken than I have on a few high-quality sets still in rotation now. I urge you to invest in the best you can afford. Here are my top picks for lunch packing gear.

LUNCHBOXES

Stainless steel bento boxes are my top choice because of their durability (they are indestructible), ease of care (can be cleaned in the dishwasher), and versatility: The divided trays of bento boxes allow you to pack a variety of foods in a single container and have versatile layouts for all kinds of meals. Also, because they are just metal, they will grow with children into adolescence while also being perfect for adults. (And they can always be dressed up with fun decals or magnets to appeal to kids if need be, without you having to compromise on the quality of the lunch gear.)

My top pick in this category is the brand LunchBots, which makes a variety of sizes and configurations of bento boxes and are the boxes we use daily. Aside from a few superficial scratches, the boxes I bought a decade ago look just as good as the new ones coming off the factory floor.

A great budget option comes from the supermarket house brand President's Choice, which makes a stainless tray topped with a plastic lid. The lids must be handwashed and are not as durable as stainless steel, but their lunchboxes are a quarter of the cost of the stainless steel alternatives. This is a great option if you have a child with a tendency to lose things—though, remarkably, this is the only lunchbox my kids have ever lost at school!

SALAD AND NOODLE BOWL CONTAINERS

There are some great options on the market that are geared to adults packing lunch on the go. Look for something that is watertight to contain sauces and dressings, is dishwasher-safe, and can, ideally, be popped into the microwave for warm meals.

Glass food-storage containers are always a great option for salads and warm meals and are available everywhere at all price points. LunchBots makes fantastic stainless steel salad bowls in a variety of sizes. Porter has a line of beautiful ceramic bowls and gorgeous glass jars that can all go in the microwave.

THERMAL CONTAINERS

A high-quality thermal container makes all the difference between a hot and lukewarm meal. I prefer widemouth containers because they are easy to fill, eat from, and then clean. I pack everything—broths, soups, stews, meatballs, dumplings, spring rolls, and other hot food items—in them.

My top picks in this category are from S'well, which makes a great container in several sizes and beautiful designs that hold heat very well, and from LunchBots, whose containers hold heat exceptionally well and have a brilliant pressure-release button that allows you to break the seal that can form on other containers and make it very difficult to open a container full of hot food. The LunchBots containers are also dishwasher-safe, which is something I appreciate for the times my kids have forgotten their dirty lunch gear in their school bags over a long weekend and eventually brought them home with new creatures growing inside of them! Another brand to look for is Stanley, which has been around for more than a century and makes durable and high-quality thermal food jars that are a little more budget-friendly.

LUNCH BAGS

It's good practice to pack your lunchbox or bowl into a bag—not only for convenience, but also so that you can pop a cold pack into the bag for food that needs to stay cold and because the bag can help contain any leaks. Buy a lunch bag that can be washed, ideally in the washing machine, and then hung to dry. I don't invest in expensive bags because they do wear out, or worse, can absorb a pungent smell from a leak that cannot be washed out and then have to be replaced. The one exception to my rule is Pack-It's line of lunch bags with integrated ice packs. Pop one in the freezer at least 12 hours before intended use and it will do a great job keeping food cold—a good solution for hot days when safe food storage is a concern.

DRINKING BOTTLES

A good thermal bottle will keep cold things cold and hot things hot. I like to pack infused water on hot days and warming broths on cold days, so I count on high-quality thermal bottles to keep things at the right temperature. I am a fan of the widemouth S'well bottles because they are easy to clean, but there are lots of great options on the market. A funnel—either a narrow or wide-mouth canning one—is handy when filling up a bottle with a smoothie or hot soup. And the scrubbing brushes that look like pipe cleaners are good for cleaning out the straws and other components of the lids.

CUTLERY

It's my experience that cutlery goes missing all the time, so I have a bunch of mismatched sets including inexpensive cocktail spoons and forks from the dollar store that won't leave me heartbroken when they don't make it home.

ACCESSORIES

I use little jam jars or other small containers from the dollar store, supermarket, or home goods store for salad dressing and other condiments, and I find silicone muffin cups are useful for further dividing a bento box or keeping foods separated.

PREPPING YOUR KITCHEN

Having a well-planned kitchen space is key for stress-free mornings. When we moved into our current home more than a decade ago, I discovered to my horror that while the kitchen seemed bigger than my old kitchen, there was much less storage space. I pared down our accumulated kitchen gear to only what I truly needed, and I have not missed a thing since. Get your gear in order and you'll thank yourself later! Below are the items I cannot live without.

The other part of the equation is making sure you have the ingredients and supplies you need on hand. Having a well-stocked pantry, fridge, and freezer (which I think of as my frozen pantry) is half the battle when preparing and making lunch.

BAKEWARE: Muffin pan; mini loaf pan; various cake pans; baking sheets in quarter and half sizes; a few round cookie cutters; measuring spoons and cups.

CHEF'S KNIFE: My favorite knife and the one I use most often is a santoku-style chef's knife that I purchased at the supermarket for about $40. I bring it to a commercial kitchen supply store for sharpening a few times a year and it is a delight to use.

COOKWARE: Small and medium saucepans, Dutch oven or other large pot for soup or pasta, large skillet, small and large nonstick skillets, panini/grill pan.

CUTTING BOARD: Buy the largest cutting board you can find so that you can chop food and just slide it across the board until you are ready to use it. The board I have on my counter at all times is intended for carving meat and has a gutter around the perimeter that comes in handy for catching liquids or keeping eggs from rolling away. Large cutting boards are not inexpensive, but they will last a lifetime. Be sure to oil and wax them regularly to keep them in tip-top shape and to stop them from absorbing odors from onions, garlic, and more.

MISCELLANEOUS TOOLS: Silicone spatulas for everything; Microplane for garlic, ginger, and parmesan; vegetable peeler; melon baller; sieve and colander for draining or sifting.

SMALL APPLIANCES: High-speed blender, immersion blender, food processor, electric kettle, waffle iron, panini press.

TOASTER OVEN: Not only did my new kitchen not have as much storage as my last kitchen, but it also didn't have a built-in microwave—something I didn't notice until we were unpacking! We had a spot in our pantry that was big enough for either a small microwave or large convection toaster oven, and I chose the latter. I use it every single day for making toast, melting cheese, baking frozen lunch items, or even baking a dozen muffins. I added a microwave when we did a little remodel, but the toaster oven is still the star of the kitchen!

PANTRY

- **BAKING SUPPLIES**: Flour (all-purpose and whole wheat), brown and granulated sugar, baking powder, baking soda, chocolate chips.
- **CANNED AND JARRED GOODS**: Chickpeas, black beans, cannellini beans, tomatoes, tomato sauce and paste, roasted red peppers.
- **CONDIMENTS**: Jams and jellies, tahini, vegetable and meat stock concentrates.
- **GRAINS, NOODLES, AND PASTA**: Quinoa, farro, barley, selection of short- and long-grain rice, assortment of pasta shapes.
- **OILS AND VINEGARS**: Extra virgin olive oil, grapeseed oil, toasted sesame oil, balsamic vinegar, white balsamic vinegar, red and white wine vinegar, rice wine vinegar.
- **SEEDS, DRIED FRUIT, AND OTHER SNACK-ING SUPPLIES**: Pumpkin seeds, sunflower seeds, chia seeds, flax, raisins, dried cranberries, apples, and apricots.
- **SPICES**: Kosher salt, cinnamon, dried ginger, turmeric, cardamom, cumin, caraway seeds, chili powder, various chili

peppers and peppercorns, spice mixes (like Moroccan mix or za'atar).

FRIDGE

- **CHEESE**: Look for packages of real (not processed) sliced cheese in the deli section of the supermarket; they are fantastically convenient for throwing together quick sandwiches and come in a wide range of varieties. I also keep blocks of our favorite cheeses in the fridge for slicing ourselves, as well as containers of ricotta (for batches of lemon ricotta pancakes see page 40) and cream cheese (for a bagel or even a quick smoked salmon tortilla rollup for when we're feeling indulgent). Truth be told though, I add to my cart anything else that jumps out at me at the store (my husband and eldest daughter love cheese!).
- **OTHER DAIRY**: Butter (unsalted for baking, salted for eating!), heavy cream, milk (we drink 1% and I bake with whole milk or pea protein and oat milk when making things dairy-free), yogurt, labneh.
- **CONDIMENTS**: My fridge overflows with opened condiments (and my pantry with the ones we haven't opened yet!). They include a selection for sandwiches, like basil and sundried tomato pesto, squeeze bottles of aioli, various chutneys, mustards, and hot sauces.
- **DIPS**: Hummus, guacamole, salsa.
- **FRESH FRUITS**: Both these, and fresh vegetables, are great for snacking or as an addition to any lunchbox, e.g., berries, apples, oranges, mangoes, pineapple, melon.

- **FRESH VEGETABLES**: Baby carrots, cucumbers, little sweet peppers, celery, jicama.
- **PROTEINS**: Eggs, tofu (blocks and packages of marinated tofu), and meat options like grilled chicken to top salads or a selection of sliced deli meats for quick sandwiches or antipasto lunches.

FREEZER

- **BREAD PRODUCTS**: Sourdough and whole wheat loaves, pita, bagels, buns, wheat tortillas, naan. (Note: Do not freeze corn tortillas because they will turn to mush when you defrost them!)
- **COOKED GRAINS AND RICE**: Grains and rice freeze well—cool them before storing them in an airtight container or bag— and can be quickly thawed for a grain bowl or even popped, still frozen, into a pot of soup. Neither are difficult to make but both can be time-consuming, so it is handy to have them prepared for when you are pressed for time.
- **COOKED MEATS AND POULTRY**: I usually pick up a few extra portions of meat or poultry so that when I am roasting, barbecuing, or smoking I have some leftovers to either pack into a container or vacuum seal. I use this meat to top a rice or noodle bowl, add to a hearty salad, or pack into a sandwich.
- **FROZEN FRUITS**: Bags of fruit for smoothies and baking.
- **FROZEN VEGETABLES**: Bags of frozen edamame (both shelled and unshelled to quickly cook and pack for lunch or snacks), corn, sweet peas, squash, and sweet potato to toss in a pan for beefing up a salad or for a pot of vegetable soup.
- **PREPARED FOODS**: Dumplings, samosas, spanakopita, bourekas.
- **PUFF PASTRY** (when you get to the handpie recipes on page 149, you'll know why!).

INGREDIENT PREFERENCES

For the recipes in this book, unless otherwise stated:

- **SALT**: Kosher (I use Diamond Kosher Salt which has large flakes; if you're using a brand with smaller flakes, reduce the quantity called for in the recipe)

- **PEPPER**: Freshly ground black

- **OLIVE OIL**: Extra virgin (I buy whatever is on sale and use it for most of my cooking, salad dressings, etc.)

- **BUTTER**: Unsalted

- **EGGS**: Large

- **MILK**: Low-fat (but whole for baking)

- **PARMESAN**: Fresh (I use a Microplane for really finely grated, fluffy cheese)

- **HERBS AND GINGER**: Fresh

- **MEAT AND FISH**: If you can, find a good local butcher and fishmonger to buy from, they can be a great source of information and inspiration

PACKING YOUR LUNCHBOX

Even after years of documenting packed lunches, talking about lunches casually with friends, and answering questions on lunches in newspapers, on the radio, and on TV, I still spend the first week of September wondering how I am ever going to manage to pack 190+ of them (x2) in the school year to come. After the first few days (and a few moments of forced meditation/ deep breathing in front of my fridge), I always go back to the same strategies (see pages 5 to 8), and, I always keep this high-level lunchbox plan in mind to help me think about the who, what, why, and how of packing lunchboxes.

WHO

Think about who you are packing for, whether it's for yourself or for others, and what they most like to eat midday. While I love to regularly introduce new foods to my children, I don't ever do this at lunchtime because it's more important for lunch to nourish them for an afternoon of school than to expand their culinary horizons. Or, for me, if I were still at a particular office job with a strict no-smelly lunch (or popcorn!) policy, I'd resist packing anything overly fragrant—no one likes that person in the open-plan office with the funky feast!

WHAT AND WHY

I loosely reference recommended food guides for guidance on what to pack for lunch. I'm looking for lunches that are balanced between food groups and that will provide the nutrients and fuel needed for the long stretch between lunch and dinner. That means something:

- **SATISFYING:** Meat, eggs, tofu, yogurt, cheese, beans, etc.
- **STARCHY AND FILLING:** Grains, noodles, rice, bread or crackers, etc.
- **CRUNCHY AND FRESH:** Raw, steamed, or roasted vegetables
- **SWEET:** Fruit and/or a baked treat

Sometimes some of these components are combined in a grain bowl; other times they're wrapped up together in tofu and vegetable dumplings; and yet other times I'll make sure the veg component is covered with a side of raw vegetable sticks and a dip. However it comes together, I try to check off each of these categories on my mental lunch packing list.

HOW

The logistics of how to get lunches from your kitchen counter into your lunchbox really has an impact on how much the food will be enjoyed come lunchtime. These may be less exciting but are important details of how to pack a lunch:

KEEP HOT FOOD HOT: Pack hot food in a pre-warmed thermos (filling the thermos with hot water while you prep lunch is a good way to do this) or in a microwave-safe container so that it can be warmed up again before eating.

KEEP COLD FOOD COLD: Pack food that must stay cold with an ice pack. Even better, pack food that must stay cold the night before, and put the whole lunchbox in the fridge (then add an ice pack in the morning before you go).

AVOID SOGGINESS: Allow items like pastries, samosas, egg rolls, or panini-style grilled sandwiches to cool down before packing them, to prevent them from getting soggy in your lunchbox.

FRESHNESS FIRST: Separate sandwiches, waffles, pancakes, or any of the warm items noted directly above with some parchment paper or reusable wax wrap, or in a sealed-off section of your lunchbox, to keep them nice and fresh.

LEAK PREVENTION: If you are using a bento-style lunchbox that has a divider but is not sealed at the bottom (like the LunchBots bentos), line sections with parchment paper or reusable wax wrap or use a silicone cup to contain anything that could leak from one section to another (like juicy fruit). Similarly (and this I share from experience!), be sure to seal off sections containing salads or sushi that you will drizzle dressing or soy sauce over from other sections to prevent anything from migrating over to the fruit or muffin you have packed!

MAKE IT PRETTY!

You know what they say, we eat with our eyes first, so presentation is really key. The quickest and easiest route to making your lunch look gorgeous is to inject it with color and texture! Add some colorful carrots, a few mini sweet peppers, some cucumber sticks, and some berries alongside a sandwich; add color to a green salad with ribbons of zucchini, carrot, radish; add a handful of fresh herbs alongside a handpie for a beautiful edible canvas (and some variety for your taste buds).

NOTE: *Look at the packing tips and photos that accompany the recipes in the book to help inspire your lunch packing adventures!*

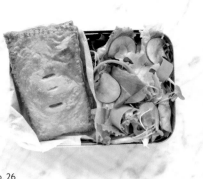

BRUNCH
FOR LUNCH

BACON & EGG HANDPIES

MAKES: 4 SMALL HANDPIES; 2 SERVINGS   **ACTIVE TIME:** 10 MINS   **TOTAL TIME:** 30 MINS

We entertain family and friends regularly, and while we usually end up having guests over for dinner, I actually love to invite people over for brunch even more. A weekend brunch is relaxed, the food is comforting and easy, and you can wear your favorite soft and stretchy clothes! Carry this carefree vibe over to the work and school week by packing brunch for lunch. These bacon and egg handpies are my youngest daughter's favorite recipe, and one that she volunteers to sample for quality control regularly. They are one of many handpie recipes in this book—take a look at Handpies 101 (page 149) for an illustrated step-by-step guide, and get ready to stock you freezer with boxes of puff pastry.

GET AHEAD: These handpies can be prepared ahead of time, see page 149 for your options.

3 eggs

2 Tbsp heavy cream

Salt and pepper

2 tsp butter

3 strips bacon, cooked and crumbled

¼ cup shredded sharp cheddar

1 recipe Handpies 101 (page 149)

NOTE

Make these handpies vegetarian by leaving out the bacon and swapping in some diced sundried tomatoes or sautéed mushrooms instead.

1. Preheat the oven to 420°F and line a baking sheet with parchment paper.

2. In a bowl, lightly beat the eggs. Add the cream and a pinch of salt and pepper, and whisk to combine.

3. In a small skillet over medium heat, melt the butter. Pour in the egg and cream mixture. Using a rubber spatula, stir the eggs and cook until barely set—you want soft curds, but no liquidy bits (you will be baking the eggs later once they are wrapped in pastry to fully cook). Take the pan off the heat and mix in the crumbled bacon and shredded cheese.

4. Let the filling cool down for a few minutes as you prepare the pastry and set things up to bake. Turn to page 150 for the filling, wrapping, baking, and packing directions for your handpies.

PACKING TIP: Complement this rich pastry with a green salad tossed with a bright vinaigrette like the Bright Green Dressing (page 108) or White Balsamic & Parmesan Dressing (page 113).

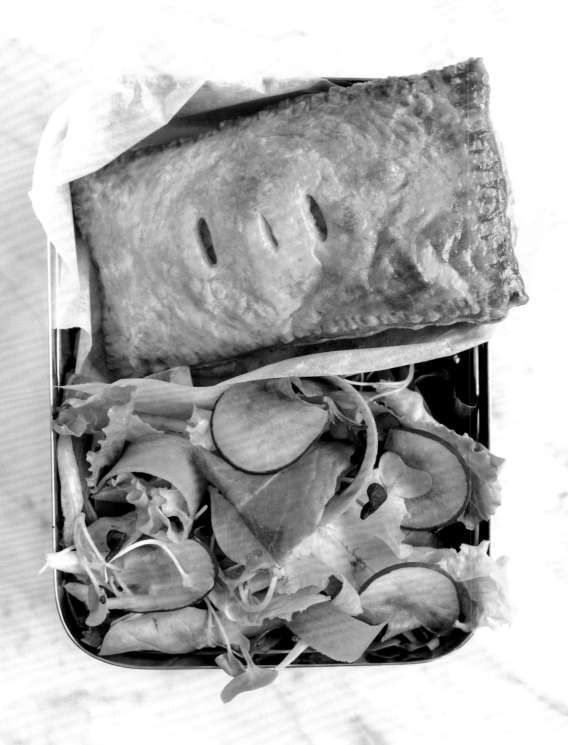

EGG IN A ROLL

MAKES: 2 SERVINGS   **ACTIVE TIME:** 5 MINS   **TOTAL TIME:** 30 MINS

I can remember learning how to make egg in a hole over a campfire at sleepover camp. Carefully balancing a cutting board on our knees, we'd place a slice of bread on top and use a juice glass to cut a circle out of the middle of it. The bread slices were then carefully lowered into a pan on the fire and an egg cracked into each hole. Given all this was happening while sitting lakeside, it makes for a very special food memory! My husband and I met at camp, so we made sure to pass this food tradition along to our girls, who regularly eat egg in a hole for breakfast or as an after school snack. This recipe, for egg in a *roll*, is a more filling spin on our camp favorite and is sure to carry you through the afternoon.

GET AHEAD: Make this recipe the morning of, so they're still nice and fresh at lunchtime. The prep time is so minimal, though (especially if you buy pre-sliced cheese), that you can make them in your PJs, and then hop in the shower as they bake.

2 crusty rolls

4 slices cheese (like havarti, sharp cheddar, or gruyère)

2 eggs

1 green onion or a few chives, thinly sliced

Salt and pepper

1. Preheat the oven to 350°F and line a baking sheet with parchment paper or foil.

2. Using a pointed serrated knife, like a steak knife, cut out a cavity from the top of each roll, taking care not to perforate the bottom. Line the cavity of each roll with two slices of cheese. If the cheese is not flexible, pop the rolls (with cheese) onto the baking sheet and into the preheating oven for a minute or two so that the cheese becomes pliable and will more easily line the cavity.

3. Carefully crack an egg into each cavity, scatter some green onions overtop, and season with salt and pepper. Bake for 20 to 25 minutes, until the egg is fully cooked. If you are serving immediately, feel free to leave the yolk runny, but cook it through if you are packing it for later in the day.

PACKING TIP: Pack this tasty egg in a roll with a crunchy slaw. You can shred some cabbage, kale, or kohlrabi yourself, or buy a bag of shredded vegetables to save time, and toss them with a drizzle of oil and vinegar (or even better, the dressing for the superfood slaw on page 61).

EGG, GREENS, & CHEESE TORTILLA

MAKES: 2 SERVINGS   **ACTIVE TIME:** 10 MINS   **TOTAL TIME:** 10 MINS

This quick and easy egg and tortilla rollup is equally tasty warm out of the pan or sliced up and packed in a lunchbox. Don't hesitate to play around with the filling based on what you have in the fridge. More often than not, I grate up odds and ends from my cheese drawer and throw in a handful of greens that are a bit too wilted to eat raw but are perfectly good to eat warmed.

GET AHEAD: This quick and easy recipe is best made the day of, but luckily it can be quickly thrown together between sips of coffee and bites of breakfast.

2 tsp butter

4 eggs, lightly beaten with a pinch of salt

2 large (8- to 10-inch) flour tortillas

2 handfuls baby spinach

½ cup shredded gruyère or any other hard cheese that melts nicely

1. Make the tortillas one at a time. In a medium nonstick pan over medium heat, melt half of the butter. Add half of the beaten eggs and immediately top with a tortilla, pressing it down gently so that some of the egg flows up and over the top side of the tortilla.

2. Cook for 1 minute and then top with half of the spinach and cheese. Cover the pan and cook for 2 more minutes, until the greens have wilted and the cheese has melted.

3. Next, either fold the eggy tortilla up in the pan, the way you would an omelet, and pack for lunch as is, or slide it out onto the cutting board and allow it to cool for a few minutes. Repeat the process for the second tortilla. Once cool, roll up the tortillas, and slice into pieces as needed to fit in your lunchbox.

PACKING TIP: Pack the tortilla with your favorite condiment—like salsa, hot sauce, or ketchup—and add a side of roasted potatoes and some sweet berries to create that authentic brunch-for-lunch feeling.

GREAT FOR KIDS: Slice the rolled tortilla into rounds and secure with some fun food picks to make this wholesome lunch a kid-friendly finger food.

SWEET POTATO & ONION FRITTATA

MAKES: 2 SERVINGS   **ACTIVE TIME**: 15 MINS   **TOTAL TIME**: 35 MINS

Frittata, the baked cousin of the omelet, is delicious to eat for lunch alongside a salad or on a crusty roll with some garlicky mayonnaise and cheese. It is a fantastic vehicle for odds and ends in the fridge—leftover roasted vegetables, a handful of greens, a mixture of shredded cheeses, etc.—and, if this wasn't enough, it also freezes beautifully in portions!

GET AHEAD: This frittata can be made ahead and stored in the fridge for up to 3 days, or freezer for up to 3 months. It's tasty at room temperature or warmed up, so it's a great lunch at your desk or on the go. The Maple, Onion, & Thyme Jam (page 188) can be made up to a week ahead of time.

2 Tbsp olive oil, plus extra for brushing the loaf pan

1 cup peeled and ¼-inch-diced sweet potato

Salt and pepper

¼ cup Maple, Onion, & Thyme Jam (see page 188)

⅓ cup crumbled herb-coated goat cheese

6 eggs, lightly beaten

NOTE

For even cooking, this frittata is baked in a water bath, where the pan that the eggs are in nests inside a larger pan filled with hot water. It is a bit fiddly but yields the best and tastiest results, so it's worth the extra effort and care.

1. In a large skillet over medium heat, heat the olive oil. When the oil begins to shimmer, add the sweet potato, a big pinch of salt and a grind of pepper. Cook, stirring occasionally, until the sweet potato has softened and is taking on some color, about 12 minutes. (If you just took the jam out of the fridge, it may have solidified; add it to the warm pan to loosen up for a minute.)

2. Meanwhile, preheat the oven to 375°F, and boil a kettle of water (see Note). Brush the sides of a 9 × 5-inch loaf pan with olive oil and line with parchment paper (this makes it easier to remove the frittata once it's cooked). Place this loaf pan into a larger (8 × 10-inch or bigger) baking dish or roasting pan.

3. Spread the onion and sweet potato mixture into the loaf pan and sprinkle with the goat cheese. Carefully pour in the eggs.

CONTINUES

4. Pull out the middle oven rack, and place the baking dish on it. Carefully pour the boiled water into the space between the loaf pan and the baking dish so that it comes about halfway up the loaf pan. Don't panic if you accidentally splash a bit of water into the eggs—it will evaporate and your frittata will still be delicious! Carefully push the rack back in and close the oven door. Bake for 20 to 25 minutes, until the eggs are set and golden.

5. Carefully remove the loaf pan from the oven (leaving the larger one, filled with hot water, to cool in the oven until it's safe to handle). Allow the frittata to cool in the pan for about 10 minutes, then slice into two portions; I vary the shape depending on how I choose to serve it.

PACKING TIP: Pack the frittata with some crusty bread and a green salad, or make it a breakfast sandwich by packing it on a crusty roll spread with some garlic mayonnaise. Some fresh fruit or veg goes great on the side.

GREAT FOR KIDS: Cut the frittata into small squares pierced with a fun food pick to make frittata finger food!

PUMPKIN SPICE WAFFLES

MAKES: 6 WAFFLES; 2 SERVINGS   **ACTIVE TIME:** 15 MINS   **TOTAL TIME:** 30 MINS

In the November of the year I turned 14 years old, I was thrilled to get a job at a newly opened frozen yogurt store (as a means to fund my love for acid-wash jeans and oversized sweaters). Given it was winter in Toronto (not peak season for a frozen dessert store!), I found myself with plenty of time on my hands to experiment with all kinds of sweet treats. One of the things I most loved to make were Belgian waffles. They smelled intoxicating and there was something magical about pouring some batter into a waffle iron, closing the lid, and opening it a few minutes later to find a gorgeous golden waffle.

These pumpkin spice waffles are significantly more wholesome than the ones I used to make at the store, but they are equally magical and delicious, especially packed for lunch with a tub of yogurt and some fruit. And don't despair if you haven't got a waffle iron! You can use this batter to make pancakes that are just as delicious.

GET AHEAD: These waffles can be made ahead and stored in the fridge for a few days, or freezer for up to 3 months. Just pop frozen waffles into the toaster for about 5 minutes to revive them.

½ cup all-purpose flour

¼ cup whole wheat flour

1 tsp baking powder

½ tsp baking soda

1 tsp pumpkin spice

¼ tsp salt

½ cup milk

¾ cup sweet potato or butternut squash purée (see Note)

2 Tbsp melted butter, cooled

1 Tbsp brown sugar

1 egg, white and yolk separated

Cooking spray, for your waffle iron

1. Set up your waffle iron according to the instructions; I like to place the iron on top of a baking sheet or a kitchen towel to catch any drips.

2. In a large bowl, combine the flours, baking powder, baking soda, pumpkin spice, and salt. Use a whisk to mix everything together and break up any clumps of flour.

3. In a medium bowl, combine the milk, sweet potato purée, butter, brown sugar, and egg yolk. Use your whisk to mix together.

4. Place the egg white in a medium bowl and use a clean whisk or a hand mixer to beat until firm peaks form.

CONTINUES

Sweet potato and butternut squash purées are available in cans at the supermarket, but you can easily make your own. To do so, peel and dice 2 medium sweet potatoes into 1-inch cubes (or peel, seed and dice 1 small butternut squash into the same size); toss with some grapeseed or other neutral oil, and roast in a 400°F oven for 30 to 45 minutes, until browned at the edges and soft. Remove from the oven, mash with a fork until smooth, and store in an airtight container in the fridge for up to 5 days.

5. Add the sweet potato purée mixture to the dry ingredients and use a rubber spatula to combine. When combined, carefully fold in the stiff egg white.

6. Follow the instructions for your waffle iron to cook six waffles, spraying the waffle iron with cooking spray between batches. Allow the waffles to cool to room temperature before packing for lunch.

PACKING TIP: I like to pack these waffles with a side of maple syrup–sweetened Greek yogurt dusted with cinnamon, and some sliced apples and pomegranate arils. On chilly days, a thermos of warmed applesauce instead of the sliced apples will be sure to hit the spot!

GREAT FOR KIDS: Make waffles a handheld food by packing them as a waffle sandwich! Swap out the bread in your child's favorite sandwich and use these lightly sweetened waffles instead. They are delicious with sunflower butter and banana, cream cheese and jam, or sharp cheddar and chutney.

INFALLIBLE CREPES

MAKES: 6 CREPES; 2 SERVINGS   **ACTIVE TIME:** 15 MINS   **TOTAL TIME:** 15 MINS

While true crepes are not difficult to make, they are a bit delicate for a packed lunch. This no-fail recipe uses a flour tortilla as its base and produces a heartier but no less delicious "crepe"—essentially a tortilla French toast—in minutes. Fill your crepes with any number of savory or sweet fillings—whatever you have in the fridge and whatever you are craving.

GET AHEAD: These crepes are best enjoyed the day they're made, but you can prepare your fillings the night before for a quick morning turnaround (see Note).

4 eggs

2 Tbsp heavy cream

Pinch salt

½ tsp vanilla (sweet crepes only)

2 tsp granulated sugar (sweet crepes only)

Butter, for cooking

6 small flour tortillas

Your choice of fillings (see Note)

NOTE

My suggestions for savory filling options include grated gruyère with baby spinach and a pinch of nutmeg; grated cheddar with sautéed mushrooms; or smoked salmon, cream cheese, and dill. For sweet crepes, I like mixed berries, ricotta, and lemon zest; banana slices and shaved chocolate; or sautéed apples with cinnamon.

1. Crack the eggs into a large bowl or onto a large rimmed plate and add the cream and salt (plus the vanilla and sugar if you are making sweet crepes). Using a fork or a whisk, mix everything together, breaking up the eggs and combining everything until the mixture is uniformly yellow.

2. Heat a nonstick skillet over medium heat and add a knob of butter. While the butter melts, dip a tortilla in the egg mixture and flip it over to coat it.

3. Transfer the tortilla to the pan and cook for 2 to 3 minutes, until the edges are browning and the bottom has browned, then flip to cook the other side. Transfer to a plate to cool and repeat the process with the remaining tortillas.

4. Place the fillings of your choice in the center of each cooked crepe, roll or fold it up, and pack it for lunch.

PACKING TIP: Pack savory crepes with a simple green salad, or try the Cucumber, Dill, & Yogurt Salad (page 110). Add an extra serving of sweet fruit alongside sweet crepes and a serving of Maple Seed Brittle (page 207) for a decadent midday meal.

LEMON RICOTTA PANCAKES

MAKES: ABOUT 8 (4-INCH) PANCAKES; 2 SERVINGS   **ACTIVE TIME:** 10 MINS   **TOTAL TIME:** 15 MINS

I discovered about a decade ago that one of the best ricotta manufacturers in the city is just minutes from my house, situated along a funny semi-industrial stretch of businesses surrounded by a residential neighborhood. There is a little shop inside their factory where you can purchase large containers of fresh hot ricotta and where I have been known to line up with a dozen elderly Italian men first thing in the morning to get our fresh ricotta fix. Fresh ricotta is a magical thing, but if you can't get your hands on any, use the best whole-milk ricotta you can find. I routinely double this recipe and freeze what I don't pack for lunch, so that I have a stash of pancakes on hand at all times.

GET AHEAD: These pancakes freeze beautifully, so make them ahead of time and store in the freezer for up to 3 months. Pop frozen pancakes into the toaster for a few minutes to thaw, and then into your lunchbox.

¾ cup whole-milk ricotta

2 eggs

¼ cup milk

I tsp vanilla

Zest of 2 lemons

Juice of I lemon (zest it before you juice it!)

I Tbsp melted butter, cooled

¼ cup granulated sugar

¾ cup all-purpose flour

I tsp baking powder

¼ tsp salt

Butter, for cooking

1. In a large bowl, combine the ricotta, eggs, milk, vanilla, lemon zest and juice, butter, and sugar. Whisk together until smooth and you have broken up any lumps of ricotta.

2. In a medium bowl, mix the flour, baking powder, and salt together, then add to the ricotta mixture. Switch your whisk for a rubber spatula and mix the dry ingredients in until you have a uniform batter.

3. Heat a large nonstick skillet over medium heat. Add a knob of butter. Once it has melted, scoop about ¼ cup of batter and pour it into the pan. Depending on the size of your pan, you should be able to fit about three pancakes in the pan at a time.

4. After 4 or 5 minutes, when the edges are browned and little bubbles have formed on the surface, flip the pancakes and cook for about another 2 minutes, until golden. Transfer the pancakes to a cooling rack and allow to cool to room temperature before packing.

PACKING TIP: Pack with fresh fruit and berries. Top your pancakes with a dusting of icing sugar and some lemon rind and fresh mint to garnish.

GREAT FOR KIDS: Transform these pancakes into "pacos"— pancake tacos—by tucking berries into folded pancakes for little hands.

BASIC CRUNCHY GRANOLA

MAKES: 4 CUPS   **ACTIVE TIME:** 10 MINS   **TOTAL TIME:** 35 MINS

I love to start my day with a bowl of yogurt and berry-topped granola, and from a young age my kids have enjoyed a granola parfait for lunch or as an after-school snack. Granola is so easy and inexpensive to make at home and allows you to add your favorite mix of seeds, dried fruit, and more. Treat this recipe as a blank canvas and add whatever ingredients you have in your pantry, or anything that jumps out at you while grocery shopping. Keep a batch on hand for days when you just have a few minutes to throw together something for lunch, to avoid a disappointing fast-food alternative.

GET AHEAD: This granola can be made ahead and stored at room temperature for up to 1 month, or in the freezer for up to 3 months.

2½ cups rolled oats

¼ cup whole flax seeds

¼ cup pumpkin seeds

¼ cup raisins

¼ cup dried cranberries

½ cup grapeseed or sunflower oil

½ cup honey or other liquid sweetener

NOTE

Dried apples, apricots, cherries, and figs are all lovely additions to granola. Sunflower and sesame seeds, as well as cacao nibs and hemp hearts, will add crunch to your cereal bowl. Add the cacao nibs and hemp hearts after baking, as they can become bitter when baked.

1. Preheat the oven to 325°F and line a rimmed baking sheet with parchment paper.

2. In a large bowl, combine the oats, flax seeds, pumpkin seeds, raisins, and cranberries. Pour in the oil and honey and stir together to evenly coat.

3. Tip the mixture onto the prepared baking sheet and spread out evenly. Bake for 25 minutes, stirring halfway through and keeping an eye on it during the last 5 minutes to be sure the dried fruit does not burn. Remove from the oven when the granola is caramel brown. It will crisp up as it cools. Allow to cool before storing in an airtight container.

PACKING TIP: Pack a generous scoop of granola alongside some yogurt and berries or other fresh fruit. If you don't have to be mindful of nuts, top it with roasted walnuts, pecans, or sliced almonds too.

p. 47

p. 48

p. 51

p. 52

p. 55

p. 56

p. 59

p. 61

p. 65

SANDWICHES

ASPARAGUS FRITTATA ON BRIOCHE

MAKES: 2 SANDWICHES **ACTIVE TIME:** 10 MINS **TOTAL TIME:** 25 MINS

I am a creature of habit and tend to order exactly the same thing when I visit one of our regular restaurants. This asparagus frittata sandwich was my order every single time we picked up a meal at a paninoteca just along the street from our house—until they tragically removed it from the menu! I miss it, but have done my best to make my own version so I can still enjoy the wonderful combination of asparagus, egg, and sundried tomato.

GET AHEAD: The frittata can be made ahead and stored tightly wrapped in the fridge for up to 2 days. Assemble your sandwich the night before (and store in the fridge) or day of.

8 to 10 asparagus spears, tough ends removed and trimmed to a max of 8 inches in length

Olive oil

Salt

4 eggs, lightly beaten

2 Tbsp heavy cream

1 tsp fresh thyme leaves

1 Tbsp chopped green onions

2 brioche buns, halved and lightly toasted

3 Tbsp Sundried Tomato Pesto (page 185)

2 slices provolone

1. Preheat the oven to 350°F.

2. Place the asparagus in an 8-inch square baking pan, drizzle with some olive oil and sprinkle with salt, and toss to coat. Roast in the oven for 5 minutes. Remove from the oven and carefully brush some olive oil about 1 inch up the sides of the pan.

3. In a medium bowl, whisk together the eggs, cream, thyme, green onions, and a big pinch of salt. Pour over the asparagus and bake for 12 to 15 minutes, until puffed up, cooked through, and slightly browned at the edges. Remove from the oven and set aside to cool. When cooled, cut into quarters.

4. Place two quarters of frittata on the base of each bun, then top each with half of the cheese, half of the pesto, and the top of each bun.

PACKING TIP: Pair this indulgent sandwich with a bright green salad with a peppy vinaigrette, like my White Balsamic & Parmesan Dressing (page 113). This sandwich is delicious enjoyed cool as well as warmed up before eating.

NOTE

If asparagus is not in season, substitute a big handful of baby spinach and skip the initial roasting step. For a flavor boost, add 3 tablespoons diced pancetta to the egg mixture.

EXCEPTIONAL EGG SALAD SANDWICH

MAKES: 2 SANDWICHES   **ACTIVE TIME:** 10 MINS   **TOTAL TIME:** 10 MINS + BOILING EGGS

When our eldest daughter was a baby, my mother would come over and take care of her for a few hours on a Saturday afternoon so that we could go and spend some baby-free time (and then spend all of it talking about our baby!). We usually ended up at a local café, and one afternoon in what must have been the haze of sleep deprivation, I ordered an egg salad sandwich on sourdough. Until that moment, I absolutely detested egg salad and would choose to not eat at all if egg salad was the only option, but this bright and herby sandwich changed my life and inspired this recipe. Instead of sourdough, I have suggested using a softer pullman bread and have tucked a halved egg into the center of the sandwich in the style of a tamago sando, a Japanese egg sandwich; it will reveal itself like a sunny smile when you slice the sandwich in half.

GET AHEAD: This recipe calls for cooled, hard-boiled eggs. Boil your eggs in advance and store them unpeeled in a bowl, or peeled in the fridge for up to 5 days. Hard-boiled eggs may also be available in the dairy section of your supermarket and are a great time-saver.

¼ cup mayonnaise

¼ tsp very finely chopped or Microplaned garlic

Lemon wedge

¼ cup finely chopped fresh dill

I green onion, finely chopped

½ tsp salt

Pepper

4 hard-boiled eggs, cooled and peeled

4 slices pullman or other sandwich bread

1. In a medium bowl, use a rubber spatula to combine the mayonnaise, garlic, and a squeeze of lemon juice. Add the dill, green onions, salt, and a grind of pepper and stir again to combine the herbs into the garlicky mayonnaise.

2. Cut one of the four hard-boiled eggs in half lengthwise and set it aside. Place the other three eggs in a bowl and mash them up with a potato masher or pastry blender. Add the mashed eggs to the herb and mayonnaise mixture and stir to combine. Have a taste and add an extra squeeze of lemon juice or salt and pepper as needed.

3. Set out the four slices of bread in two rows of two in front of you. Place one half of the reserved hard-boiled egg in the center of each of two of the slices and top each with half of the egg salad mixture. Top with the other slice of bread and cut in half widthwise to serve.

PACKING TIP: Wrap the sandwiches in waxed paper or pack in an airtight container. Keep them refrigerated or packed with an ice pack until eaten. Pack this sandwich with some crunchy vegetable sticks and Roasted Red Pepper Spread (page 189), if you like dipping your veg.

GRILLED BROCCOLI, MOZZARELLA, & ROASTED RED PEPPER ON FOCACCIA

MAKES: 2 SANDWICHES   **ACTIVE TIME:** 15 MINS   **TOTAL TIME:** 15 MINS + MAKING DIP

Hearty vegetarian sandwiches can be hard to come by, but this one—probably my favorite sandwich of all time—breaks the mold. Grilled broccoli is robust in both flavor and texture and is perfectly paired here with creamy fresh mozzarella and savory Roasted Red Pepper Spread.

GET AHEAD: This sandwich can be made the night before but is best the day it is prepared. The recipe calls for some of the Roasted Red Pepper Spread (page 189); make this delicious spread a few days ahead, reserve what you need for the sandwich, and toss the rest with some roasted potatoes for a quick and easy side dish at dinner.

2 cups large broccoli florets, sliced in half lengthwise

Olive oil, for drizzling

Salt and pepper

2 (4-inch) squares focaccia

4 Tbsp Roasted Red Pepper Spread (page 189)

1 (6 to 8 oz) ball fresh mozzarella, sliced

Chili flakes (optional)

1. Place the broccoli florets in a microwave-safe bowl, cover with a lid, and microwave on high for 3 minutes. Remove the bowl from the microwave and tip the broccoli out onto a clean kitchen towel to dry.

2. Preheat your panini pan on high heat. While the pan is heating, place the broccoli back into the bowl and toss with a drizzle of olive oil and some salt and pepper. When the pan is hot, add the broccoli and cook on each side for about 2 minutes, until there are dark brown grill marks. Set aside to cool.

3. Slice the focaccia in half crosswise. Spread each piece with roasted red pepper spread. Put half of the mozzarella on the bottom half of each focaccia and top it with the grilled broccoli. Season with salt and pepper, add a few chili flakes if you like some heat, and close up each sandwich with the top half of the focaccia.

PACKING TIP: Wrap or pack in an airtight container. If you store these in the fridge, allow to warm up for a few minutes before eating. This sandwich has it all—protein, vegetables, and lovely bread—so just pack it with some fresh fruit to round out your meal.

GOAT CHEESE, PEACH, & BASIL PANINI

MAKES: 2 SANDWICHES   **ACTIVE TIME:** 15 MINS   **TOTAL TIME:** 15 MINS

I bought our panini pan—a rectangular grill pan with a matching rectangular lid that sits inside the pan—in the clearance section of a department store years and years ago, but it wasn't until we had kids that I put it to use on a weekly basis. Quick grilled sandwiches are not only delicious but incredibly versatile—and, it turns out, very practical because they hold together in your lunchbox no matter how much you might throw your school bag around in the yard before going to the classroom for the day! This combination of peach and goat cheese is my eldest daughter's favorite and this is the sandwich that she takes on the first day of school every single year. The start of the school year coincides with the height of peach season, but for all those times when local fruit is not available, I buy imported peaches and grill them on the panini pan before assembling the sandwich, to bring out their peachy sweetness.

GET AHEAD: This sandwich is best the day it is prepared, but thanks to its simplicity, it can be thrown together quickly and popped into your panini pan between mouthfuls of breakfast.

2 peaches, halved and pitted

4 oz soft fresh goat cheese

4 slices pullman or other soft grilling bread

Handful fresh basil leaves or 4 Tbsp basil pesto

NOTE

To make a kohlrabi slaw, peel and grate I or 2 bulbs of kohlrabi using the coarsest side of a box grater until you have about 2 cups. Toss with the juice of ½ a lime, I thinly sliced green onion (green parts only), I tablespoon of sesame oil, and a big pinch of salt. Add a sprinkle of roasted sesame seeds on top for added flavor.

1. Preheat your panini pan on medium-high heat.

2. While the pan is warming up, thinly slice the peaches. Spread the goat cheese on two slices of the bread and top with the peach slices. If using fresh basil, give it a rough chop and divide it between the two sandwiches. If using pesto, spread it on the other two slices of bread and place atop the peaches and goat cheese.

3. Transfer the sandwiches to the panini pan and grill for 3 to 4 minutes on each side, until the cheese has softened and there are nice dark caramel-brown grill marks on the bread.

4. Remove from the pan and allow to cool before slicing and packing. The sandwiches can be popped into a toaster oven to be revived when needed, or eaten at room temperature.

PACKING TIP: Pack this sandwich in an airtight container with some fresh fruit a quick and easy kohlrabi slaw (see Note) for a lovely, light end-of-summer meal. Kohlrabi is a member of the brassica family and has a pleasant crispy texture and slightly sweet flavor.

SMOKED CHEDDAR, APPLE, & SPINACH PANINI

MAKES: 2 SANDWICHES   **ACTIVE TIME:** 15 MINS   **TOTAL TIME:** 15 MINS

This sandwich combines sweet, salty, smoky, and creamy flavors—and a handful of greens!—all in between two slices of bread. What could be better? This recipe calls for a few tablespoons of Fig & Balsamic Onion Jam (page 186), a simple one-pot jam recipe that pairs well with charcuterie and cheese and is well worth keeping at the back of your fridge. It does not take long to make, but do plan ahead to speed up lunch packing.

GET AHEAD: Make the (fabulously delicious) Fig & Balsamic Onion Jam (page 186) in advance and store in the fridge for up to 1 week. This sandwich is best served the day it is made, but can be revived quickly in a toaster oven before eating, if you decide to make it in advance.

1 large apple, halved and cored

4 oz shredded smoked cheddar

4 slices hearty whole grain bread

Handful baby spinach

4 Tbsp Fig & Balsamic Onion Jam (page 186)

1. Preheat your panini pan on medium-high heat.

2. While the pan is warming up, thinly slice the apples. Divide the shredded cheese between two slices of bread. Top the cheese with spinach and then layer the apple slices on top. Spread 2 tablespoons jam on each of the other two slices of bread and place atop the cheese, spinach, and apples.

3. Transfer the sandwiches to the panini pan and grill each side for 3 to 4 minutes, until there are some nice grill marks, the cheese has melted, and the spinach has wilted.

4. Remove from the pan and allow to cool before slicing and packing.

PACKING TIP: This sandwich is in regular rotation in our house in the fall—especially after we have been apple picking—and it pairs well with a lovely warming fall soup. Pack it alongside a thermos of Curried Leek & Potato Soup (page 85) and some fresh fruit for a perfect fall lunch, sure to warm you from the inside out.

GRUYÈRE & PEAR SANDWICH

MAKES: 2 SANDWICHES   **ACTIVE TIME:** 5 MINS   **TOTAL TIME:** 5 MINS

On a weekend away in New York City, my husband and I stopped and had a bite of lunch at one of those corporate expense–account sorts of restaurants near Central Park. We normally try to track down something more exciting, and the details of why and how we ended up at this place are hazy—we must have been starving, or perhaps the weather was terrible—but what I do remember distinctly is the sandwich I ate for lunch! It was a wonderful gruyère, pear, frisée, and caramelized onion sandwich on sourdough that I have subsequently recreated many times in my own kitchen. I'm sure it will hit the spot for you too.

GET AHEAD: This sandwich is best served the day it is made, but be sure to make the Maple, Onion, & Thyme Jam (page 188) in advance—not only for this sandwich, but also for the Potato, Cheddar, & Bacon Flatbread in the next chapter (page 76).

4 Tbsp Maple, Onion, & Thyme Jam (page 188)

4 slices sourdough bread, lightly toasted

4 oz sliced gruyère

2 pears, halved, cored, and thinly sliced

A few frisée leaves or other bitter greens

1 Tbsp Dijon mustard

1. Spread the jam on two slices of the bread, then top with the cheese, pears, and frisée. Spread the Dijon mustard on the other two slices of bread, then place atop the fillings, mustard side down, to close up the sandwiches. Slice in half if desired.

PACKING TIP: I love a sandwich with a bowl of soup at midday! Pack this sandwich with a thermos of Carrot & Orange Soup (page 82) or Roasted Butternut Squash Soup (page 86) for a wonderfully satisfying lunch.

NOTE

If your pears aren't quite ripe or aren't especially flavorful, halve and core them, put a little knob of butter on each one, and pop them onto a baking sheet. Roast them in the oven at 400°F for 15 minutes, until softened, and allow to cool before adding them to your sandwich.

SOURDOUGH CROSTINI WITH RICOTTA, PEARS, HONEY, & THYME

MAKES: 2 SANDWICHES   **ACTIVE TIME:** 15 MINS   **TOTAL TIME:** 15 MINS

What makes this recipe so wonderful is its simplicity, and the key to the best result is to use the best ricotta and baguette you can get your hands on. Fresh ricotta is ideal, but any whole-milk ricotta will do the trick. Between this and the pears, lemon, honey, and thyme, you will have a luxurious and satisfying lunch. These crostini are also great with drinks in the garden or around the fire on chilly winter days.

GET AHEAD: This recipe should be put together the morning of, but the different components can be made ahead and stored in separate containers until you need them: the crostini at room temperature for several days; the cheese mixture in the fridge for up to 3 days; the pears in the fridge for a day or two.

8 (I-inch) slices sourdough baguette

Olive oil

Salt

2 pears, peeled, quartered, and cored

Honey

3 sprigs fresh thyme

I cup whole-milk ricotta

Zest of I lemon

NOTE

If great pears are not available, peaches, apricots, nectarines, and even blueberries are yummy alternatives.

1. Preheat the broiler to low and locate a baking sheet. Do not line the baking sheet with parchment paper—it could catch fire under the broiler! You can line it with foil to save cleanup time or leave it as is and wipe it down after.

2. Brush both sides of the baguette slices with some olive oil and place on the baking sheet. Sprinkle each with a bit of salt. Pop under the broiler and keep an eye on them while you toast both sides until medium brown and crisp, about 2 minutes on each side. Remove from the oven, keeping the broiler on, and transfer the crostini to a cooling rack to cool before packing.

3. Place the pear quarters on the baking sheet and drizzle with a bit of honey and olive oil. Pop under the broiler and broil until the pears have softened a bit and the edges have started to brown, about 4 minutes. Remove from the oven and set aside to cool. When cooled, sprinkle with the leaves from one sprig of thyme.

CONTINUES

4. In a small bowl, mix the ricotta, lemon zest, a drizzle of olive oil, the leaves from the two remaining sprigs of thyme, and a pinch of salt.

5. To eat, top each crostini with a scoop of the ricotta mixture, a wedge of pear, and, if you are feeling fancy, an extra drizzle of honey.

PACKING TIP: Pack the crostini, pears and ricotta separately in your lunchbox, and put them together as you eat. They pair well with a hearty green salad dressed with White Balsamic & Parmesan Dressing (page 113).

CHICKEN OR TOFU KATSU SANDWICH

MAKES: 2 SANDWICHES **ACTIVE TIME:** 15 MINS **TOTAL TIME:** 25 OR 35 MINS

Nothing beats crispy and crunchy breaded chicken topped with a vinegary but slightly creamy slaw on a soft and slightly sweet bun, but tofu is a great substitute, and it pleases both the vegetarians and the meat eaters in my house. You can either pan-fry or bake this recipe; fried is crispier but requires more attention and a fussier cleanup. This recipe calls for a bag of super-food greens—the mix of kale, red cabbage, and other chopped hearty greens that is available in the produce section of the supermarket. Feel free to substitute any mix of greens in its place.

GET AHEAD: This sandwich is best the day it is made, but you can make the chicken or tofu a day or two in advance and store it, well wrapped, in the fridge. Crisp it up again in the toaster oven or in a pan with a bit of oil over medium heat. The slaw will keep in the fridge for up to 2 days.

½ cup panko

1 Tbsp sesame seeds

1 tsp salt

2 boneless, skinless chicken thighs or ½ block firm tofu, cut into 2 slices

1 egg, lightly beaten

Cooking spray

Grapeseed or other neutral oil (if frying)

2 brioche buns

SLAW

3 green onions, green parts only, cut into thirds

Juice of 1 lime

1 small clove garlic

3 Tbsp mayonnaise

Salt and pepper

Pinch chili flakes (optional)

1 small bag superfood greens

2 Tbsp toasted sunflower seeds

1. If you are baking the chicken or tofu, preheat the oven to 425°F and line a baking sheet with parchment paper. If you are frying, have a baking sheet or large plate ready to place the coated chicken or tofu on before frying.

2. Dry off the chicken or tofu with a paper towel. In a medium bowl, mix the panko, sesame seeds, and salt. Dip the first chicken thigh or piece of tofu into the beaten egg and then into the panko mix, coating on all sides. Place on the prepared baking sheet or plate. Repeat with the remaining chicken or tofu.

3. If baking, spray the chicken or tofu generously with cooking spray on all sides, then place in the oven for 20 to 25 minutes, until the coating is golden and crispy and an instant-read thermometer inserted in the thickest part of the chicken registers 165°F. If frying, heat about ¼-inch grapeseed oil in a skillet over medium heat; place the chicken or tofu in the warm skillet and cook on both sides until golden brown and crispy—about 7 to 8 minutes per side.

CONTINUES

To make this sandwich vegan, use dairy-free milk in place of the egg, vegan mayonnaise in place of regular, and a crusty roll if you cannot find a vegan brioche.

4. While the chicken or tofu cooks, place the green onions, lime juice, garlic, mayonnaise, a big pinch of salt, a few grinds of pepper, and a pinch of chili flakes (if you like a bit of heat) in a small blender or a tall jar suitable for use with an immersion blender. Blend for about a minute, until you have a bright green dressing. Taste and add more salt and pepper if needed. Place the superfood greens mix in a bowl, pour the dressing overtop, and toss to coat. Sprinkle the sunflower seeds over the top of the slaw.

5. When the crispy chicken or tofu is ready, remove from the oven or skillet, transfer to a cooling rack to cool for about 10 minutes, then place in the brioche buns. Top the sandwich with a generous scoop of slaw right before eating.

PACKING TIP: Pack the sandwich in your lunchbox, with the slaw in an airtight container on the side. I usually pack some orange wedges too for a sweet and light conclusion to this yummy lunch.

CURRIED CHICKEN SALAD SANDWICH

MAKES: 2 SANDWICHES   **ACTIVE TIME:** 15 MINS   **TOTAL TIME:** 15 MINS

This curried chicken salad is a throwback to one of my favorite warm-weather meals that my mother used to make. She would use leftover chicken in her version of this curried chicken salad and serve it as part of a cold meal on warm days. To tell the truth, I liked the leftover salad more than the chicken she made originally! Something about the combination of chicken, crispy sweet apple, and celery tossed together in a curried tangy sauce is so moreish. Who knows, maybe like 10-year-old me, you'll also want to skip dinner in favor of more of this salad?

GET AHEAD: Whip up this chicken salad the night before and assemble your sandwich in the morning. Use leftover chicken from dinner (try grilling a couple extra breasts or thighs), or buy a roasted whole chicken or legs.

¼ cup plain Greek yogurt

½ cup mayonnaise

1 tsp yellow curry paste

Juice of ½ lime

Salt and pepper

1½ cups diced cooked chicken

½ cup ¼-inch-diced celery

½ cup ¼-inch-diced apple

2 green onions, thinly sliced

4 slices whole grain sourdough bread

Handful baby spinach or
   other greens (optional)

NOTE

You can pack this chicken salad on a bed of greens instead of on bread if you prefer. If packing this for a nut-friendly environment, add a handful of toasted walnuts for an added crunch.

1. Mix the yogurt, mayonnaise, curry paste, lime juice, and a pinch of salt together in a medium bowl until you have a gorgeous golden mixture. Add the chicken, celery, apple, and green onions. Using a rubber spatula, fold everything together until well coated. Have a quick taste and add salt or pepper if needed.

2. Top 2 slices of the bread with half of the chicken salad and half of the baby spinach. Top each with the other slices of bread and cut in half.

PACKING TIP: This sandwich is lovely packed alongside a quick mango chaat. To make one: very thinly slice a ripe mango, top it with some pomegranate arils, a squeeze of lime juice, a big pinch of chaat masala (a delicious addition if you have some on hand), some chopped cilantro, and some crunchy (nut-free if needed) Mumbai or dal mix. Mumbai and dal mixes (as well as chaat masala) are available in the Indian food section or snack section of the supermarket, and, of course, at Indian food stores.

p. 68

p. 71

p. 72

p. 75

p. 76

FLATBREADS

GRAPE, FETA, KALE, & ROSEMARY FLATBREAD

MAKES: 2 SERVINGS   **ACTIVE TIME:** 5 MINS   **TOTAL TIME:** 10 MINS

Naan, the oven-baked flatbread that is a staple of Indian cuisine, is widely available at the supermarket. It is richer and more delicate than pita and the perfect base for a quick and easy lunchbox flatbread. This flatbread has a combination of sweet, salty, and tangy flavors, topped with a virtuous sprinkle of kale—does it get any better?

GET AHEAD: This flatbread is best the day it is prepared, but the Fig & Balsamic Onion Jam (page 186) should be made ahead and stored in the fridge for up to 5 days.

2 naan, each about 8 inches long

¼ cup Fig & Balsamic Onion Jam (page 186)

1 cup shredded kale

Pepper

½ cup halved seedless red grapes

½ cup crumbled feta

1 sprig rosemary, leaves only, finely chopped

1. Line a baking sheet with foil and turn the broiler in your oven to low.

2. On each naan, spread half of the fig and balsamic onion jam, and top with the shredded kale and a few grinds of pepper. Sprinkle on the grapes, feta, and chopped rosemary.

3. Place the prepared naan on the baking sheet and pop under the broiler until the kale has wilted and the cheese has softened, about 3 to 4 minutes. Remove from the oven and allow to cool before packing for lunch. The flatbread is best warm or at room temperature.

PACKING TIP: Slice up some extra kale and pack yourself a quick and easy side salad to accompany this flatbread. Make a delicious dressing with the Fig & Balsamic Onion Jam (page 186) to drizzle over top of the kale, and add a handful of sunflower and pumpkin seeds and a tablespoon of sliced green onion, for some added crunch and flavor.

HEIRLOOM TOMATO, CORN, & PESTO FLATBREAD

MAKES: 2 SERVINGS   **ACTIVE TIME:** 10 MINS   **TOTAL TIME:** 15 MINS

Corn and tomatoes are a match made in heaven, and even more so when they are in season! This flatbread celebrates their pairing, adding some pesto and mozzarella for good measure. If fresh corn is not available, don't hesitate to substitute frozen corn.

GET AHEAD: This flatbread tastes best the day it is prepared, but it can be made ahead and stored in the fridge for up to 2 days.

1 Tbsp grapeseed oil (or other neutral oil suitable for high heat)

1 ear corn, kernels removed (about ¾ cup)

Salt and pepper

2 naan, each about 8 inches long

¼ cup Deep Green Fall Pesto (page 184)

½ cup shredded mozzarella

2 large or 3 medium tomatoes (heirloom varieties if available), cut into ½-inch slices

1. Preheat the oven to 375°F and line a baking sheet with foil or parchment paper.

2. In a skillet over medium-high heat, warm the oil. (I'd recommend you turn on the exhaust fan because the charring corn may set off your smoke detector.) When the oil shimmers, add the corn, sprinkle on some salt and pepper, and cook, stirring often, until the kernels begin to char. Remove from heat and set aside. (Alternatively, you can char the corn—kernels still on the cob—on your grill outdoors, then remove the kernels once it has cooled.)

3. Place the naan on the prepared baking sheet. Spread the pesto on both of the naan, then add the corn and top with the shredded cheese, tomato slices, and some salt and pepper. Pop into the oven for about 10 minutes, until the cheese has melted and sections of the cheese and naan have started to brown. Remove from the oven and allow to cool down before packing for lunch. Best enjoyed at room temperature.

PACKING TIP: Pack with fresh fruit and a decadent Baked Chocolate Banana Donut (page 206) for a sweet and delicious treat.

GRILLED ZUCCHINI, PRESERVED LEMON, & HERB FLATBREAD

MAKES: 2 SERVINGS   **ACTIVE TIME:** 10 MINS   **TOTAL TIME:** 10 MINS

This flatbread reminds me of the thin-crust pizzas topped with a mountain of salad greens that popped up in the early 2000s and that I could not get enough of! There was something so wonderful about the combination of the soft and pliable crust folded around greens. I have updated it here with ribbons of zucchini tossed in a zippy preserved-lemon dressing.

GET AHEAD: The zucchini topping can be made ahead and stored in the fridge for up to 2 days.

2 naan, each about 8 inches long

2 medium zucchini, sliced into thin ribbons with a vegetable peeler or mandoline

3 Tbsp olive oil

Salt and pepper

½ cup mixed chopped fresh herbs (one or all of basil, mint, dill, thyme, and parsley)

Zest of 1 lemon

2 Tbsp finely chopped preserved lemon, seeds removed first

1 Tbsp lemon juice

1. Warm a grill pan (or a cast-iron pan if you haven't got a grill pan) over medium-high heat. Grill both sides of the naan until they have dark brown grill marks on each side, about 2 minutes per side. Remove from the pan and allow to cool before popping into a lunchbox. Leave the heat on under the pan because you will be cooking the zucchini momentarily.

2. In a bowl, toss the zucchini ribbons with 1 tablespoon olive oil and some salt and pepper. Transfer the ribbons to your grill pan and cook for about 1 to 2 minutes on each side, until the zucchini have grill marks and have softened. Keep an eye on the zucchini while it cooks, especially while cooking the second side, because it will cook quickly. Return the zucchini to the bowl and allow to cool. Once cooled, toss with the herbs and lemon zest.

3. Using a small blender or immersion blender, blend the remaining 2 tablespoons olive oil, and the preserved lemon, lemon juice, and a pinch of salt and pepper together until smooth. Pour over the grilled zucchini and herbs and toss to coat.

PACKING TIP: Pack the dressed zucchini in an airtight container. When ready to eat, top the grilled naan with the zucchini. This is best served at room temperature. Pack a simple, sweet dessert of grilled stone fruit, yogurt sweetened with honey, and some fresh mint.

NOTE

Preserved lemons—lemons that are brined with salt and spices—are readily available at Middle Eastern grocers and in some large supermarkets. My favorite are from a local business that makes them in small batches and with significantly less salt than the shelf-stable variety. I highly recommend tracking down similar ones if you can.

BUTTERNUT SQUASH, LEEK, GOAT CHEESE, & PESTO FLATBREAD

MAKES: 2 SERVINGS   **ACTIVE TIME:** 15 MINS   **TOTAL TIME:** 30 MINS

This flatbread is a scaled-down version of a crowd-sized nibble that I used to make for the moms and babies (and then toddlers!) group in my neighborhood. The women who gathered each week were a terrific source of support and friendship, and, to my delight, they all loved to cook and eat. Some of us are still in touch, and in awe that our babies are now nearly old enough to drive! To make a crowd-sized version of this flatbread, pick up a prepared pizza crust or a delicious Persian Barbari, quadruple the toppings and extend the cooking time to about 30 minutes.

GET AHEAD: This flatbread can be made ahead of time and stored in the fridge for up to 2 days.

I Tbsp olive oil

I cup peeled and ½-inch-diced butternut squash

½ cup finely sliced leek, light parts only

Salt and pepper

I small package (4oz) goat cheese, crumbled

I egg, lightly whisked

3 Tbsp Deep Green Fall Pesto (page 206)

2 naan, each about 8 inches long

1. Preheat the oven to 375°F and line a baking sheet with foil or parchment paper.

2. In a skillet over medium heat, warm the olive oil. When it shimmers, add the squash and leek, season with salt and pepper, and cook until the leek has wilted and the squash has softened, about 7 minutes. Set aside to cool.

3. Add the goat cheese and egg to a bowl and season with a generous pinch of salt and a few grinds of pepper. Stir together until smooth.

4. Place the naan on the prepared baking sheet and spread half of the cheese and egg mixture on top of each one. Top each with the cooked squash and leek. Bake in the oven for 15 minutes, until the cheese mixture is golden and set.

5. Remove from the oven and allow to cool for a few minutes before garnishing with dollops of pesto. Enjoy warm or at room temperature.

PACKING TIP: There's a nice variety of vegetables on this flatbread, so pack it with a simple serving of crunchy fruit; it pairs especially well with pears, one of my favorite fall fruits.

POTATO, CHEDDAR, & BACON FLATBREAD

MAKES: 2 SERVINGS   **ACTIVE TIME:** 10 MINS   **TOTAL TIME:** 35 MINS

Bread and potatoes are among my favorite foods, and when combined they only serve to elevate each other! This decadent flatbread, with its smoky, sweet, and tangy flavors, pairs well with a crisp green salad or some crispy raw vegetables for lunch.

GET AHEAD: This recipe is best enjoyed the day it is made, but you can prepare the potato and bacon the night before, for a quicker turnaround in the morning. The Maple, Onion, & Thyme Jam (page 188) should be made in advance and stored in the fridge for up to 5 days. Short on time? Substitute it with some caramelized onions or store-bought onion jam instead.

1 small unpeeled potato, thinly sliced (about ⅛- to ⅟₁₆-inch slices)

1 tsp olive oil

1 small sprig rosemary, leaves only, chopped

Salt and pepper

2 naan, each about 8 inches long

½ cup Maple, Onion, & Thyme Jam (page 188)

2 strips bacon, cooked until crispy and crumbled

½ cup shredded sharp cheddar

NOTE

Leave out the bacon to make this flatbread vegetarian and substitute smoked cheddar for the cheddar called for in the ingredients list to keep some of its smoky flavor.

1. Preheat the oven to 425°F and line a baking sheet with parchment paper.

2. In a bowl, toss the potato slices with the olive oil, rosemary, some salt, and a few grinds of pepper. Spread the slices out on the baking sheet and roast for 15 minutes, until the edges of the potatoes begin to brown and small golden-brown patches appear on the surface of the slices. (This is also a good time to cook the bacon if you haven't already.) Remove the baking sheet from the oven and set it aside.

3. Divide and spread out the potato slices on the two naan. Top with the maple, onion, and thyme jam and the crumbled bacon. Sprinkle the cheddar on top, then transfer the prepared naan to the baking sheet you used for the potatoes. Bake for 10 minutes, until the cheese has melted, is bubbling away, and is beginning to brown in spots.

4. Remove from the oven and allow to cool before slicing and packing for lunch. Enjoy either warm or at room temperature.

PACKING TIP: Pack this indulgent flatbread with a selection of raw vegetables and a container of Roasted Red Pepper Spread (page 189) for dipping—it's the perfect light, spiced foil for the rich flavors of the flatbread.

p. 81

p. 82

p. 85

p. 86

p. 89

p. 90

p. 93

p. 95

SOUPS

ROASTED TOMATO SOUP

MAKES: ABOUT 4 CUPS; 2 SERVINGS   **ACTIVE TIME:** 15 MINS   **TOTAL TIME:** 40 MINS

My family never tires of tomato soup. This one is magically creamy—even in the absence of cream—thanks to some roasted sweet potato blended in with the tomatoes. I love to pack this for lunch on chilly days alongside a grilled cheese sandwich or some grilled cheese soldiers for my kids. Winter tomatoes can be a little tasteless, so I use cherry tomatoes, but you could also substitute a can of whole tomatoes.

GET AHEAD: This soup can be made ahead and stored in the fridge for up to 5 days, or in the freezer for up to 3 months.

2 cups halved cherry tomatoes

2 shallots, peeled and quartered

½ cup peeled and ½-inch-diced sweet potatoes

Olive oil, for drizzling

Salt and pepper

2 Tbsp olive oil

I clove garlic, thinly sliced

Pinch chili flakes

2 cups vegetable or chicken stock

Basil leaves, for garnish

1. Preheat the oven to 400°F and line a small baking sheet with parchment paper.

2. In a bowl, toss the cherry tomatoes, shallots, and sweet potatoes with a drizzle of olive oil and a generous pinch of salt. Tip out onto the baking sheet and roast for 25 to 30 minutes, until the tomatoes and sweet potatoes have started to brown around the edges.

3. In a medium saucepan over medium heat, heat the 2 tablespoons olive oil until it shimmers. Add the garlic and chili flakes and cook for a minute or two, until your kitchen is filled with the smell of garlic. Add the roasted vegetables and stock and simmer for about 15 minutes, until the sweet potatoes have softened enough that you can mash them against the side of the pot.

4. Purée the soup in a blender or using an immersion blender. Taste and season with salt and pepper if needed. Garnish with basil leaves.

PACKING TIP: Is there anything better than tomato soup with a grilled cheese sandwich? Pack this soup hot in a pre-warmed thermos (see page 22) along with a simple grilled cheese—I like cheddar in between two slices of Pullman's loaf bread—cut into two for yourself (or into strips for kids who like to dip!).

CARROT & ORANGE SOUP

MAKES: ABOUT 4 CUPS; 2 SERVINGS   **ACTIVE TIME:** 15 MINS   **TOTAL TIME:** 35 MINS

This simple and satisfying soup uses two of my favorite winter ingredients: carrots and oranges. It's a lovely cool-weather lunch that warms you from the inside out, thanks to the sunny orange and earthy cumin and coriander.

GET AHEAD: This soup is quick enough to make the morning of, but can be made ahead and stored in the fridge for up to 5 days, or freezer for up to 3 months.

2 Tbsp butter or olive oil

I onion, diced

4 cups peeled and coarsely chopped carrots

2 tsp ground coriander

I tsp ground cumin

4 cups vegetable or chicken stock

I cup orange juice

Salt and pepper

1. In a medium saucepan over medium heat, melt the butter. Add the onions and cook, stirring occasionally with a rubber spatula, for about 7 or 8 minutes, until the onions are translucent and have started to brown.

2. Add the carrots, coriander, and cumin and cook, stirring, until the spices are fragrant, about 2 minutes.

3. Add the stock and bring to a boil. Reduce the heat and allow to simmer until the carrots are soft (you should be able to easily mash one with a fork), about 20 minutes.

4. In a blender or using an immersion blender, purée the soup until smooth. Add the orange juice, stir, and taste. Season with salt and pepper as needed.

PACKING TIP: Pack the soup hot, in a pre-warmed thermos (see page 22) garnished with cilantro. Make it a hearty lunch by adding some grilled naan or pita and some Hummus (see page 183), along with a quick chopped salad of whatever crunchy vegetables you have in the fridge—top them with chickpeas, a generous drizzle of olive oil, a squeeze of lemon juice, and salt and pepper.

CURRIED LEEK & POTATO SOUP

MAKES: ABOUT 4 CUPS; 2 SERVINGS   **ACTIVE TIME:** 15 MINS   **TOTAL TIME:** 35 MINS

We accumulate a stockpile of potatoes in the fall from our farm-box delivery, and while I probably couldn't ever tire of eating crispy roasted potatoes, it is nice to change things up a bit. When we received a couple of enormous leeks one week, I decided to whip up a pot of leek and potato soup. Just then, my daughter wandered into the kitchen and asked if I could make her "that" leek and potato soup—the one she had in a museum café in London 4 years earlier that tasted just like a dosa. I'm always up for a challenge, so I set about recreating the soup for her as best I could. If our food memories serve us well, this recipe captures the essence of the warming and flavorful soup she couldn't forget.

GET AHEAD: This soup can be made ahead and stored in the fridge for up to 5 days, or freezer for up to 6 months.

3 Tbsp butter or olive oil

2 cups sliced leeks, light parts only

2 large shallots, peeled and thinly sliced

3 cloves garlic, thinly sliced

2 cups peeled and ¼-inch-diced potatoes

2 to 3 Tbsp yellow curry paste (the more you use, the spicier it gets)

3 cups vegetable or chicken stock

Salt and pepper

2 Tbsp full-fat plain yogurt, or dairy-free yogurt alternative, for serving

4 tsp tamarind chutney, for serving

Lime wedges

Fresh cilantro, for garnish

1. In a large soup pot over medium-high heat, melt the butter. Add the leeks and shallots and cook, stirring occasionally with a wooden spoon or rubber spatula, until softened and translucent, about 5 to 7 minutes.

2. Add the garlic and potatoes and cook, stirring frequently, until the garlic is fragrant, about 1 minute. Add the curry paste and cook, stirring frequently, for about 1 more minute. Warning: if you're making this while hungry, the smell of the curry paste will be intoxicating!

3. Add the stock, increase the heat to high, and bring to a boil. Reduce the heat to a simmer and allow to cook, uncovered, for about 20 minutes, until the potatoes have softened.

4. If you prefer a smooth soup, purée with a blender or immersion blender; if you like it chunky, just leave as is. Taste and season with salt and pepper as needed. Serve topped with a generous tablespoon of yogurt, 2 teaspoons of tamarind chutney, and a squeeze of lime juice. Garnish with cilantro.

PACKING TIP: Pack the soup hot in a pre-warmed thermos (see page 22). Add a few samosas and a quick Kachumber salad (see Note) on the side.

ROASTED BUTTERNUT SQUASH SOUP

MAKES: ABOUT 4 CUPS; 2 SERVINGS   **ACTIVE TIME:** 30 MINS   **TOTAL TIME:** 45 MINS

About 10 years ago, my siblings and I bought a coupon from one of those group-buy websites for a private cooking lesson to celebrate my mum's birthday. These types of websites were new at the time, and things didn't quite go as planned. The night was a very memorable one for many comically or farcically bad reasons, but also one good one: we made a butternut squash bisque that included tomato juice. It seemed like such a bizarre addition before I tried it, but in fact, it made for a wonderful bisque! It inspired the inclusion of tomato paste in this recipe and in every pot of squash soup I've made since that night.

GET AHEAD: This soup can be made ahead and stored in the fridge for up to 5 days, or freezer for up to 3 months.

3 cups peeled and 1-inch-diced butternut squash

1 Tbsp olive oil

Pinch salt

1 Tbsp butter or olive oil

1 tsp ground coriander

4 cardamom pods, gently crushed but still intact

1 cup thinly sliced onions

2 cloves garlic, thinly sliced

1 tsp finely chopped ginger

3 Tbsp tomato paste

4 cups vegetable or chicken stock

Juice of 1 lime

Salt and pepper

1. Preheat the oven to 400°F and line a baking sheet with parchment paper.

2. In a medium bowl, toss the squash with the olive oil and a pinch of salt. Spread out on the baking sheet and roast for 20 to 25 minutes, until the squash has softened and starts to brown.

3. While the squash roasts, melt the butter in a medium saucepan over medium heat. Add the coriander and cardamom and cook, stirring constantly with a wooden spoon, until fragrant—about 1 minute. Add the onions, garlic, and ginger and cook for another 3 to 4 minutes. Add the tomato paste and cook, stirring, until the paste is no longer bright red but a deep brick color—about 4 minutes. Remove from heat until the squash is ready.

4. Add the roasted squash and the stock to the pan and bring to a vigorous simmer over medium-high heat. Simmer for 5 minutes, until the squash has softened completely.

5. Remove the cardamom pods from the pan (they should be floating near the surface and will have darkened in color), then use a blender or an immersion blender to purée the soup. Add the lime juice and season with salt and pepper as needed.

PACKING TIP: Pack the soup hot in a pre-warmed thermos (see page 22) topped with some pomegranate arils and fresh parsley. Serve, along with a simple ploughman's lunch: a few slices of cranberry or sourdough bread, a wedge of cheddar or blue cheese (or both!), some Maple, Onion, & Thyme Jam (page 188), and a few slices of apple.

PARMESAN BROTH WITH VEGETABLES & TORTELLINI

MAKES: ABOUT 4 CUPS; 2 SERVINGS   **ACTIVE TIME:** 10 MINS   **TOTAL TIME:** 10 MINS (+ PASTA)

This simple soup—with a vegetable-enhanced broth, some pre-cooked pasta, and a generous scoop of parmesan—comes together in under 10 minutes. It's one of the soups I love to make in early spring when I've tired of heavy-duty winter soups but still want something to warm me up from the inside out. Feel free to play around with this recipe to use whatever vegetables you have in your fridge or to sneak in a bit of leftover chicken or a handful of cooked chickpeas or beans.

GET AHEAD: This soup can be made ahead and stored in the fridge for up to 5 days. Add an extra portion of tortellini to the pot when you are making dinner and pop it into an airtight container stored in the fridge to speed up making this soup for your lunch the next day.

I Tbsp olive oil

I onion, finely diced

½ cup sliced mushrooms

½ cup finely diced carrots

½ cup finely diced celery

I clove garlic, finely chopped

3 cups vegetable or chicken stock

½ cup halved cherry tomatoes

I cup cooked mini tortellini or ravioli

¼ cup grated parmesan

Lemon wedges

1. In a medium saucepan over medium-high heat, warm the oil. When the oil shimmers, add the onions, mushrooms, carrots, and celery and cook, stirring occasionally, until the onions are translucent and the other vegetables have softened, about 5 minutes. Add the garlic and cook, stirring often, for about a minute, until the smell of garlic fills the air.

2. Pour in the stock and bring to a vigorous simmer for 3 or 4 minutes, until the carrots and celery are cooked but still have a bit of crunch. Add the cherry tomatoes and cook for 2 more minutes before turning off the heat. Stir in the cooked pasta, or pack in a separate container (see below). Enjoy topped with grated parmesan and a squeeze of lemon juice.

PACKING TIP: Pack the soup hot in a pre-warmed thermos (see page 22). The pasta in the soup has the best texture when it's added just before eating, so I pack it separately, along with the parmesan and lemon wedges. If it's easier for you, though, just add the pasta to the soup at the same time as the cherry tomatoes.

RED LENTIL SOUP

MAKES: ABOUT 4 CUPS; 2 SERVINGS   **ACTIVE TIME:** 10 MINS   **TOTAL TIME:** 35 MINS

Red lentils, unlike most legumes, cook quickly, and when combined with some basic vegetables and spices, transform into a hearty and nourishing soup. A quick note: this soup can be blended, so don't spend too much time dicing the vegetables first, just aim to cut them up evenly so they finish cooking at the same time.

GET AHEAD: This soup can be made ahead and stored in the fridge for up to 5 days, or freezer for up to 3 months. This soup thickens as it cools but will return to a soupy consistency when you warm it up again.

I Tbsp olive oil, plus more for drizzling

½ cup diced onions

½ cup diced carrots

½ cup diced celery

3 cloves garlic, finely chopped or Microplaned

2 tsp ground cumin

I cup red lentils

3 cups vegetable or chicken stock

½ lemon

Salt and pepper

Fresh parsley or cilantro, chopped, for garnish

1. In a medium saucepan or Dutch oven over medium heat, heat the olive oil. When it shimmers, add the onions, carrots, and celery and stir. Cook until the onions begin to soften and become translucent—about 10 minutes.

2. Add the garlic and cumin and cook, stirring frequently, until they are fragrant—about 1 minute.

3. Add the lentils and stock and simmer until the lentils have lost their shape and vibrant orange color; they will turn beige when fully cooked.

4. You can either stop here and enjoy a rustic bowl of soup, or you can blend the soup for a smoother and more uniform consistency. If blending, purée the soup in a blender or with an immersion blender until smooth.

5. Add a good squeeze of lemon juice. Taste and season with salt and pepper as needed. Serve garnished with a handful of chopped parsley or cilantro.

PACKING TIP: Pack the soup hot in a pre-warmed thermos (see page 22), along with some store-bought falafel (I usually have a bag in my freezer that just need to be warmed up in the toaster oven) drizzled with tahini, and some wedges of pita.

CREAMY CORN & POTATO CHOWDER

MAKES: ABOUT 4 CUPS; 2 SERVINGS   **ACTIVE TIME:** 15 MINS   **TOTAL TIME:** 25 MINS

This hearty soup comes together quickly and with simple pantry and freezer staples. It is delicious with or without cream, so feel free to omit it if you prefer a less-creamy soup. And stir in some leftover rotisserie chicken, shrimp, bacon, or even shredded smoked cheese for an even more filling midday meal.

GET AHEAD: This soup can be made ahead and stored in the fridge for up to 5 days, or freezer for up to 2 months. You may want to add a good squeeze of lime juice to wake up the flavors after storage.

I cup peeled and ¼-inch-diced potatoes

3 Tbsp olive oil

Salt

½ cup diced red onions

½ cup diced celery

I cup fresh or frozen corn kernels

2 cloves garlic, finely chopped

I tsp sweet smoked paprika

2 Tbsp white balsamic vinegar

I Tbsp fresh thyme leaves

2 cups vegetable or chicken stock

I Tbsp butter

I Tbsp all-purpose flour

¼ cup heavy cream (optional)

Juice of ½ lime

2 Tbsp chopped chives

1. Place the potatoes in a microwave-safe bowl, cover with a lid, and microwave on high for 3 minutes, until tender. Tip out onto a clean kitchen towel to dry off.

2. In a medium saucepan over medium-high heat, heat 2 tablespoons of the olive oil. Add the potatoes and a pinch of salt and cook, stirring occasionally, until the potato cubes are browned and crispy, about 5 minutes. Remove from the pan and set aside.

3. Add the remaining 1 tablespoon olive oil to the saucepan along with the red onions and celery and cook for 2 to 3 minutes, until the onions start to become translucent. Add the corn and garlic and cook for 1 minute, stirring regularly. Add the paprika and cook until fragrant, about 1 minute more.

4. Add the balsamic vinegar and, using a wooden spoon, stir and scrape up the browned bits from the bottom of the pan until the vinegar has evaporated. Add the thyme and stock and bring to a vigorous simmer; cook for 5 minutes.

CONTINUES

5. To thicken the soup, make a roux with the butter and flour: Melt the butter in a small saucepan over medium heat. When melted, add the flour and stir with a wooden spoon for about 1 minute, until the flour has cooked but has not taken on any significant color. Scoop out about ½ cup broth from the soup pan and add it to the small saucepan, stirring quickly to incorporate into the roux. Add this mixture to the simmering soup, stirring well to combine, and continue to cook until the soup has thickened, about 1 minute. Remove from heat.

6. Stir in the cream, lime juice, and chives. Taste and season with salt and pepper as needed.

PACKING TIP: Pack the chowder hot in a pre-warmed thermos (see page 22) for a wonderfully warming meal on a chilly day. Add a container of Bagel Chips (page 176), and one of Roasted Red Pepper Spread (page 189) for a dip, along with a green salad with a bright and vibrant dressing—the Bright Green Dressing (page 108) is my top choice for this.

CHICKEN SOUP

MAKES: 8 TO 10 CUPS; SERVES 4 TO 6   **ACTIVE TIME:** 30 MINS   **TOTAL TIME:** 3 HRS

About 7 or 8 years ago, my mother-in-law passed the Passover torch to me and my house took over hosting our family for the second night of this springtime Jewish holiday. Our "family" consists of about 40 people—give or take a few depending on the year—about half of whom are not technically related to us but are most definitely considered family. While my menu leans toward what's seasonal and local, chicken soup always makes the cut. After much experimentation from year to year, this is my go-to recipe that I make in vats and freeze a month or so ahead of Passover. I also make it on a regular basis throughout the year for our youngest daughter, who would happily subsist on chicken soup (and chocolate).

Good chicken soup takes time, so set aside a quiet weekend afternoon to roast the chicken and then allow the soup to bubble away on the stove for a few hours. You will be rewarded with a rich broth that will warm you from the inside out and might even magically heal a tickle in your throat or a runny nose.

GET AHEAD: This soup *must* be made ahead because of the time it simmers on the stove (see above). It can be stored in the fridge for up to 5 days, or freezer for up to 3 months. It turns to jelly when cold but returns to its regular soupy self when warmed up. If you're a bit shorter on time but still have a craving for chicken soup? Use a whole roasted chicken from the supermarket and skip the first step of the recipe.

3 lb chicken drumsticks

2 large white onions, skin on, quartered

Grapeseed or other neutral oil (like sunflower or canola)

Salt and pepper

I leek, white part only, halved lengthwise

1. Preheat the oven to 425°F. Place the chicken drumsticks and one of the quartered onions in a large roasting pan. Drizzle with oil and sprinkle liberally with salt and pepper. Use your hands to toss everything together and spread it out in the pan. Pop into the oven and roast for about 1 hour, until the chicken skin is crispy and a dark caramel color. Remove from the oven, and set aside to allow the chicken and onions to cool for about 10 or 15 minutes in the pan while you prepare the rest of the ingredients for the soup pot.

CONTINUES

2 large carrots, peeled and ends removed

2 stalks celery, halved

I small sweet potato, peeled and quartered

½ head garlic, cloves separated and skin on

¼ cup dried mushrooms

I Tbsp caraway seeds

I Tbsp coriander seeds

I tsp whole peppercorns

A few handfuls of baby spinach

Chives, finely chopped, for garnish

<u>NOTE</u>

Here is a quick recipe for a tasty batch of coleslaw. In a large bowl, use tongs to toss together 5 cups of mixed shredded cabbage and carrots, 2 chopped green onions, ¼ cup grapeseed oil, ¼ cup white vinegar, 1½ teaspoons granulated sugar, I finely grated small clove of garlic, and ½ teaspoon salt. Coleslaw improves with age, and can be stored in an airtight container in the fridge for up to 5 days.

2. In a large soup pot, combine the second quartered onion with the leeks, carrots, celery, sweet potatoes, garlic, dried mushrooms, caraway seeds, coriander seeds, and peppercorns.

3. Transfer the chicken drumsticks and onions from the roasting pan to the soup pot. Using a wooden spoon (one with a blunt end is ideal), scrape up all the roasted brown bits from the roasting pan and add them to the soup pot too.

4. Add enough cold water to the pot to cover everything by about an inch. Bring to a boil over medium-high heat, then reduce to a vigorous simmer and allow to cook away, partially covered with a lid, for 2 hours. (If you have a pressure cooker, you can cook the soup under high pressure for about 40 minutes instead, then skip ahead to step 6.)

5. After 2 hours, give the soup a stir and have a taste. If the soup has a robust chicken flavor and the broth has a deep caramel color, then it is time to strain it. If the flavor is still a bit thin, allow it to simmer for another hour before checking again.

6. When ready, strain the soup through a colander into a large bowl and optionally a second time through a sieve back into the soup pot. Set aside the meat and vegetables in the colander to cool down enough to handle. Taste the broth and season with salt and pepper as needed. If the soup still tastes a bit flat, you can give it a squeeze of lemon juice to brighten up the flavor.

7. Once the meat and vegetables in the colander have cooled down, retrieve the celery, carrots and as much meat from the drumsticks as you can. Slice the carrots into coins, shred the chicken, and add both back to the pot. Stir in the baby spinach—it will wilt instantly—and serve with a sprinkle of chives.

PACKING TIP: Pack the soup hot, in a pre-warmed thermos (see page 22), then make this a traditional deli lunch! Add a little challah roll or two, and some coleslaw. You can pick up a coleslaw at the deli counter or quickly whip up a batch at home using a bag of shredded cabbage and carrots from the supermarket (see Note).

p. 100

p. 103

p. 104

p. 107

p. 109 & 110

p. 113

p. 114

p. 117

p. 118

p. 121

p. 122

p. 125

SALADS

BEET & CITRUS SALAD

MAKES: 2 SERVINGS   **ACTIVE TIME:** 10 MINS   **TOTAL TIME:** 1 HR 10 MINS

I love to eat salads all year round, but the kind I crave changes with the seasons. This hearty roasted beet and citrus salad is perfect for winter, when beets and citrus fruit are at their prime. With a bit of planning, you can throw this salad together and be out the door in under 10 minutes!

GET AHEAD: Roast and peel your beets in advance and store them in the fridge for up to 5 days (and consider making extra—they're a great addition to any green salad). Cooked beets are also widely available at the supermarket in little vacuum-packed bags. This salad is best if put together the morning before it is eaten.

3 medium whole beets

Olive oil, for drizzling

Salt and pepper

2 cups orange, pomelo, and/or pink grapefruit segments

I small package (4 oz) goat cheese, crumbled (see Note)

2 Tbsp fresh basil ribbons and small leaves

NOTE

You can use the cheese of your choice for this recipe: feta and fresh mozzarella both pair well with beets.

1. Roast the beets: Preheat the oven to 400°F. Lay the whole beets on a 12-inch square sheet of foil. Drizzle with olive oil and sprinkle with salt. Lay another 12-inch square sheet of foil overtop and crimp the edges of the two sheets together to form a roasting envelope. Place on a baking sheet and then into the oven.

2. After about 45 minutes, carefully remove the baking sheet from the oven and peel back a corner of the foil. Insert a sharp paring knife into the center of the largest beet; if it slides in without any resistance, the beets are ready. If not, close the foil package and return to the oven, checking every 15 minutes until the beets are cooked. Remove from the oven and set aside to cool. When cooled, use your hands (I recommend wearing gloves) or a vegetable peeler to slide the skins off the beets. Slice the beets into bite-size wedges.

3. Alternate placing beet wedges and citrus segments into your lunch bowl or box. Top with the crumbled cheese and basil. Drizzle with olive oil and season with salt and pepper.

PACKING TIP: Add a couple of slices of hearty grain bread or a Pumpkin Pumpkin Seed Mini Loaf (see page 193) for a satisfying midday meal.

WATERMELON & HALLOUMI SALAD

MAKES: 2 SERVINGS   **ACTIVE TIME:** 10 MINS   **TOTAL TIME:** 10 MINS

If you haven't encountered it before, halloumi is a semi-hard, salty Cypriot cheese typically made from a mixture of goat and sheep's milk. What makes it especially magical is that, when cooked, a nice crispy crust forms on the outside, and the inside softens, but the cheese holds its shape. Halloumi pairs well with sweet, juicy watermelon in this summery salad that comes together in minutes.

GET AHEAD: The dressing can be made ahead and stored in the fridge for up to 3 days. The salad is best enjoyed the day it is made, and the cheese best served warm or at room temperature.

BASIL & MINT DRESSING

Juice of 1 lime

3 Tbsp grapeseed oil

¼ cup fresh basil leaves

¼ cup fresh mint leaves

1 tsp honey

½ jalapeno, seeds and stems removed (optional)

Olive oil, for cooking

5 oz halloumi, cut into ¼-inch cubes (see Note)

4 cups ¼-inch-cubed seedless watermelon

Fresh mint, to garnish

1. Make the dressing: In a small blender, combine the lime juice, grapeseed oil, basil and mint leaves, honey, and jalapeno (if you like a bit of heat!). Blend until smooth, about 90 seconds.

2. Warm a nonstick skillet over medium heat and add a drizzle of oil. Add the halloumi to the pan and cook on each side, turning as each side browns and crisps, 2 to 3 minutes per side. Transfer to a paper towel-lined plate.

3. In a bowl, toss the watermelon and halloumi together, then transfer to your lunch containers and pack with the dressing on the side. Dress the salad immediately before eating.

PACKING TIP: Pack this wonderful summery salad with some grilled pita, and some Maple Seed Brittle (page 207) for a sweet finish to a tasty meal.

NOTE

Some halloumi brands are saltier than others and can overpower the watermelon. Some of the best halloumi that I have found in Toronto is from Quebec; it is creamy and a bit salty, but in the best way.

VIBRANT QUINOA SALAD

MAKES: 2 SERVINGS   **ACTIVE TIME:** 10 MINS   **TOTAL TIME:** 10 MINS + COOKING QUINOA

This salad is like sunshine in a bowl! The combination of orange, orange flower water, honey, and cinnamon in the dressing is inspired by a traditional Moroccan orange salad that is typically served as a dessert. I have combined it here with quinoa, chickpeas, carrots, pickled onions, and more in a light and bright salad that is sure to turn a dreary day around. The dressing is also delicious tossed with some thinly sliced napa cabbage and green onions. Or, with a mix of baby greens, mango, and pumpkin seeds—wonderful served alongside roasted chicken.

GET AHEAD: This dressing can be made ahead and stored in the fridge for up to 5 days. The salad should be put together the day it will be eaten, but you can get a head start by cooking the quinoa and storing in the fridge for up to 5 days, or freezer for up to 3 months.

ORANGE FLOWER WATER DRESSING

⅓ cup freshly squeezed orange juice

I Tbsp lemon juice

I tsp honey or other liquid sweetener

I tsp orange flower water

½ tsp ground cinnamon

¼ tsp salt

2 Tbsp olive oil

½ tsp Dijon mustard

I cup orange segments

2 Tbsp currants or raisins

2 Tbsp Quick Pickled Onions (page 178)

I cup chickpeas

2 cups cooked quinoa

2 cups baby spinach

I cup grated carrots

2 Tbsp coarsely chopped fresh mint

1. Make the dressing: Place the dressing ingredients in a blender and run at high speed for 30 seconds to emulsify. Alternatively, place the ingredients in a lidded jar and shake it until everything is combined.

2. Pack the salad ingredients in a glass jar for the prettiest presentation, with the ingredients layered in this order: dressing, oranges, currants, pickled onions, chickpeas, quinoa, baby spinach, carrots, and mint. Give it a good shake before eating, and enjoy! Alternatively, pack the salad in a bowl (as pictured here) with the dressing in a separate container.

PACKING TIP: Pack this lovely salad with a Cranberry Orange Muffin (page 196) and a bottle of lemonade with an added splash of orange flower water (see Note).

NOTE

Orange flower water, also known as orange blossom water, is available at Middle Eastern grocery stores, large supermarkets, and online. It adds a wonderful floral flavor to the dressing. You can also try adding some to lemonade! Inspired by a drink I've had at the little meze restaurant up the street from my house, I now add I tablespoon of orange flower water to about 6 cups lemonade for a delicious warm-weather drink.

ROASTED CAULIFLOWER, MANOURI, & POMEGRANATE SALAD

MAKES: 2 SERVINGS   **ACTIVE TIME:** 10 MINS   **TOTAL TIME:** 25 MINS

Manouri is a wonderfully creamy, semi-soft Greek cheese that, magically, can be cooked in a hot pan without losing its shape. It's very mild tasting and a terrific accompaniment to the earthy roasted cauliflower and sweet and tangy pomegranate arils in this recipe. You should be able to find it at Greek markets, good cheese shops, and well-stocked supermarkets—I buy it at a Lebanese supermarket, which demonstrates its international appeal! If you can't find it, substitute a mild and creamy feta or halloumi in its place.

This is one of those salads that's as good in a bowl as it is wrapped up in a pita or some naan—I like to pack flatbread alongside it and alternate eating bites of salad folded into bread, and bites of salad from my fork! When we entertain big crowds, I like to make a blender-full of this salad's vibrant and slightly spicy Bright Green Dressing to pour over roasted vegetables or grilled fish or seafood, or to serve alongside crispy smashed potatoes. It uplifts anything it encounters and really makes food sing!

GET AHEAD: The cauliflower can be roasted in advance and stored in the fridge for up to 3 days. The dressing can be prepared up to 4 days in advance and stored the same way. The cheese is best enjoyed the day it is cooked.

I small head cauliflower, core removed and broken into florets

I Tbsp + I tsp olive oil

Salt

I (4 to 6 oz) slice manouri

½ pomegranate, arils only (about ½ cup arils)

½ cup mixed chopped fresh green herbs (some or all of parsley, mint, chives, and thyme)

1. Preheat the oven to 425°F and line a baking sheet with parchment paper.

2. In a large bowl, toss the cauliflower florets with 1 tablespoon of the olive oil and a good pinch of salt, then spread out on the baking sheet. Roast for 20 minutes, until the florets have browned in sections and are cooked through. Remove from the oven and set aside to cool.

3. Heat the remaining olive oil in a nonstick skillet over medium-high heat. Place the whole slice of manouri in the skillet and cook until browned, 2 to 3 minutes, then flip and brown the other side for another 2 to 3 minutes. Remove from heat and cut into two pieces.

CONTINUES

BRIGHT GREEN DRESSING

¼ cup grapeseed oil

¼ tsp minced garlic

I Tbsp finely diced shallots

Juice of I lime

¼ cup packed fresh cilantro stems and leaves

¼ cup packed fresh mint leaves

I Tbsp finely diced jalapeno, veins and seeds removed (see Note)

⅛ tsp salt

4. Make the dressing: Place the dressing ingredients in a small blender or a tall jar suitable for use with an immersion blender. Blend for about 90 seconds, until the ingredients are combined and you have a bright green dressing. Taste and adjust the salt and heat if necessary.

5. Make a bed of roasted cauliflower in your lunch bowl and top with the manouri, pomegranate arils, and fresh herbs. Pack the dressing on the side and drizzle when you are ready to eat.

PACKING TIP: Pack some pita or naan to enjoy alongside this delicious salad.

NOTE

Jalapenos are inconsistently spicy; some are as mild as an ordinary green pepper, while others are tear-inducing. It's easy to increase the heat in your dressing by adding a bit of jalapeno at a time, but it's impossible to reduce it, so start with a tablespoon of diced jalapeno and add a few teaspoons more as you go to reach your ideal level of spiciness.

CARROT, CURRANT, & MINT SALAD

MAKES: 2 SERVINGS　　**ACTIVE TIME:** 10 MINS　　**TOTAL TIME:** 10 MINS + CHILLING

My mother welcomes and indulges requests from her grandchildren for their favorite foods. My nephews have been known to call ahead and ask for a pot of chicken soup, and my eldest daughter has a standing order for this carrot, currant, and mint salad—lucky for my mum, this one couldn't be simpler to make! It's perfect both for a warm summer day and as a great pick-me-up in the depths of winter.

GET AHEAD: Make this salad up to 5 days in advance and store in the fridge; the flavors will benefit from the extra time. It needs at least 2 hours chilling time before serving (see Note).

---

3 cups grated carrots

½ cup dried currants

Juice of 1 orange

Juice of 1 lemon

¼ cup grapeseed or other neutral oil

¼ tsp salt

½ cup chopped fresh mint

NOTE

The salad is best served cold. Letting it rest in the fridge for at least 2 hours allows the currants to plump up and the flavors to develop. The dressing and the juices from the carrots will collect at the bottom of the bowl, so give the salad a good stir before serving.

Photo on page 111

1. In a mixing bowl, combine the carrots, currants, orange and lemon juices, oil, and salt, and use a rubber spatula to mix everything together. Fold in the chopped mint. Transfer to an airtight container and refrigerate for at least 2 hours (and up to 5 days).

PACKING TIP: There is something about this salad that reminds me of being on a picnic, so I usually pair it with the Cucumber, Dill, & Yogurt Salad (page 110)—a quick and easy salad that also tastes even better the day after you make it—and add in cubes of cheese, a wedge of baguette, and some fresh fruit.

CUCUMBER, DILL, & YOGURT SALAD

MAKES: 2 SERVINGS   **ACTIVE TIME:** 10 MINS   **TOTAL TIME:** 20 MINS

All credit for this zesty and surprisingly satisfying summer salad—one of my favorite salads of all time—goes to my mother, who has been whipping it up for picnics and warm-weather gatherings for as long as I can remember. When I called to ask her for the recipe, she revealed that it was improvised depending on the day! It's one of those things she just throws together, adding whatever herbs she has in the fridge. For the rest of us (who rely on recipes to turn out great food), here is her method and what she says is a fairly typical ingredients list.

GET AHEAD: This salad is especially good the day after it is made, so make it ahead of time and store in the fridge for up to 2 days.

2 small cucumbers, sliced into 1⁄16-inch rounds

1½ tsp salt

2 Tbsp lemon juice

½ cup whole-milk Greek yogurt or labneh

1 small clove garlic, finely minced or Microplaned

2 Tbsp olive oil

½ cup finely chopped fresh dill stems and fronds

Pepper

Lemon-infused olive oil (optional)

1. In a colander, mix the cucumber slices and salt and sit the colander on top of a bowl (or in your sink) to allow excess water to drain off for about 15 minutes. Rinse the cucumbers well with cold water, then spread them out between two clean kitchen towels to dry.

2. In a medium bowl, whisk together the lemon juice, yogurt, garlic, and olive oil. Using a rubber spatula, fold in the cucumber slices, dill, and a few grinds of pepper. Taste and season with salt and pepper as needed. Drizzle with a teaspoon or two of lemon-infused olive oil to make the salad even more luxurious.

PACKING TIP: This cucumber salad is best served cold; some liquid may separate from the cucumbers after a few hours, and you can either drain it off or just stir it back in. It pairs well with the Carrot, Currant, & Mint Salad on page 109 (as pictured here). Add in some cubes of cheese, fresh figs, and a wedge of good bread to make it a full midday meal.

KALE RIBBON SALAD

MAKES: 2 SERVINGS   **ACTIVE TIME:** 10 MINS   **TOTAL TIME:** 10 MINS

Dinosaur (or Tuscan) kale has dark green, flat leaves, and a slightly milder flavor than curly kale. Sliced in thin ribbons, it makes a lovely change from other salad greens. If you cannot find it at your greengrocer, baby kale or regular curly kale will do the trick. The dressing for this salad uses white balsamic vinegar (sometimes labeled "white balsamic condiment"), a slightly sweet and mellower relative of regular balsamic vinegar that can be found with the rest of the vinegars at the supermarket.

GET AHEAD: This salad can be made ahead and stored in the fridge for up to 4 days. The dressing will keep in the fridge for up to 3 days.

WHITE BALSAMIC & PARMESAN DRESSING

¼ cup olive oil

2 Tbsp white balsamic vinegar

¼ cup packed finely grated parmesan

⅛ tsp salt

1 bunch dinosaur kale

3 fresh figs, quartered

4 Tbsp currants

4 Tbsp pumpkin seeds

1 recipe Crispy Cannellini Beans (page 179)

1. Make the dressing: Place the dressing ingredients in a small blender or a jar suitable for use with an immersion blender. Blend for about 90 seconds, until you have a uniform golden-yellow dressing. Taste and add more salt if necessary (and a pinch of sugar or a squeeze of honey if it's tasting too acidic).

2. To prepare the kale, remove the stems from the leaves and stack the leaves on top of each other like a deck of cards. Using a sharp knife, slice thin ribbons—about ⅛ to 1/16 inch thick—across the leaves so that you are left with a pile of kale ribbons.

3. Make a bed of kale ribbons in your lunch bowl and top with the figs, currants, and pumpkin seeds. Pack the dressing on the side and toss together when ready to eat.

PACKING TIP: This bowl salad is a full meal on its own, but some you could also add some focaccia or crackers alongside.

LATE '90S SALAD

MAKES: 2 SERVINGS   **ACTIVE TIME:** 5 MINS   **TOTAL TIME:** 5 MINS

One of the great condiments to take center stage in my kitchen pantry in the 1990s was balsamic vinegar, and I ate more salads tossed with balsamic vinaigrette than I could count. While I do not miss the mesclun greens mix of that era (which invariably had a few slimy leaves hidden among the other delicate ones), I was recently happy to rediscover my fondness for a good balsamic dressing drizzled over some roasted red peppers and goat cheese. I put them all together in this tribute to '90s lunches.

GET AHEAD: This salad can be made ahead and stored in the fridge for up to 2 days. The dressing will keep in the fridge for up to 5 days.

CREAMY BALSAMIC DRESSING

¼ cup olive oil

¼ clove garlic

2 Tbsp balsamic vinegar

2 Tbsp heavy cream

2 tsp granulated sugar

⅛ tsp salt

6 cups mixed greens

2 roasted red peppers, seeds removed and cut into thin strips

4 oz fresh goat cheese, crumbled

4 Tbsp toasted sunflower seeds

4 oz grilled chicken, tofu, or other protein of your choice

1. Make the dressing: Place the dressing ingredients in a small blender or a tall jar suitable for use with an immersion blender. Blend for about 90 seconds, until all ingredients are combined and you have an unctuous and creamy consistency. Taste and adjust the salt if necessary.

2. Make a bed of greens in your lunch bowl and top with the roasted red pepper strips, crumbled goat cheese, sunflower seeds, and grilled protein. Pack the dressing on the side and toss with the salad at lunchtime.

PACKING TIP: Add some Puff Pastry Cheese Sticks (page 175) to round out your meal and to get another taste of nostalgia (is it just me who thinks of the 1970s, polyester, and wide lapels when eating those?).

SPRING CAPRESE

MAKES: 2 SERVINGS   **ACTIVE TIME:** 10 MINS   **TOTAL TIME:** 10 MINS

The arrival of asparagus is a sure sign that spring is on the way and that the cold, dark days of winter are nearly through. I can never resist buying a bunch or two, and I love to make this simple salad, a twist on the ubiquitous tomato and basil caprese, to celebrate asparagus season.

GET AHEAD: The components of this salad can all be made ahead, and then assembled the morning of. The croutons can be stored at room temperature for up to 2 weeks (make double and use them in a different salad, or in another version of this salad next week!). The dressing can be stored in the fridge for up to 1 week; the asparagus and mozzarella stored the same way for up to 2 days.

1 bunch asparagus

2 Tbsp olive oil

2 slices sourdough bread, cut into ½-inch cubes

Salt and pepper

6 oz fresh mozzarella

Handful fresh herbs (like dill, tarragon, or thyme)

LEMON GARLIC VINAIGRETTE

Juice of 1 lemon

2 tsp Dijon mustard

½ small clove garlic

½ tsp salt

½ cup olive oil

1. Bring a small pot of salted water to a boil. Slice off the tough ends of the asparagus and discard. Slice the spears into 1-inch sections and add to the pot. Cook until the asparagus are bright green and still a bit crunchy, 1 to 2 minutes. Quickly drain into a colander and rinse well under cold water to stop the cooking process. Shake off any excess water and transfer to a clean kitchen towel to dry off.

2. In a skillet over medium-high heat, warm the olive oil. Add the cubed bread, a big pinch of salt, and a few grinds of pepper. Toss in the pan and cook, giving the pan an occasional shake, until the bread has toasted on all sides and you have a pan of fresh croutons, about 5 minutes. Set aside to cool.

3. Make the dressing: In a small blender or jar, combine the lemon juice, mustard, garlic, salt, and olive oil. Process or shake until emulsified. Taste and season with salt and pepper.

4. Tear each ball of mozzarella into rough sections and toss with the asparagus in a bowl. Transfer to your lunch container and top with the fresh herbs and croutons. Pack the dressing on the side and dress immediately before eating.

PACKING TIP: Pack atop a bed of orzo for a heartier lunch, or with a wedge of crusty sourdough for a lovely light lunch.

SUMMER CAPRESE

MAKES: 2 SERVINGS   **ACTIVE TIME:** 10 MINS   **TOTAL TIME:** 20 MINS

I had grilled pineapple for the first time while visiting Tobago about 20 years ago, and it opened my eyes and tastebuds to how delicious grilled fruit can be! It enhanced the pineapple-ness of the fruit and inspired me to create this summer caprese with stone fruits. We live about 90 minutes from the Niagara Peninsula, where the most wonderful stone fruits are grown every summer. When our kids were little, we used to make an annual trip to the Niagara Parks Butterfly Conservatory and always tried to time it with the height of peach season so that we could pick up a bushel of peaches to bring home with us. We would eat them on the drive back to Toronto, grill a bunch when we got home, and then freeze the balance to pull out midwinter to remind us of those wonderful warm summer days.

GET AHEAD: This salad is best the day it is prepared and eaten at room temperature. If you know you'll be pressed for time, grill the fruit the night before and store in the fridge overnight, then assemble the salad in the morning.

2 peaches or nectarines, halved and pitted (see Note)

2 apricots, halved and pitted

Grapeseed or other neutral oil for grilling

6 oz fresh mozzarella

8 cherries, pitted

Handful fresh basil leaves, roughly torn

Olive oil, for drizzling

NOTE

Stone fruit can vary widely in size, so adjust the number of peaches or nectarines you use based on your appetite.

1. Warm up a grill pan over medium-high heat. Brush the surface of the peaches and apricots with some oil and place, cut side down, on the pan and cook until the fruit has softened and there are deep brown grill marks on the fruit, about 3 to 4 minutes. Remove from the pan and set aside to cool.

2. Tear the mozzarella into rough pieces. Slice the cooled peaches into smaller, bite-size sections. Arrange both, along with the apricots, in containers for lunch and top with the cherries, some roughly torn basil, and a drizzle of olive oil.

PACKING TIP: Pack this lovely summer salad with a Rice Pudding Muffin (page 199). These barely sweet muffins are the perfect pairing to the bright fruity flavors in the salad.

AUTUMN CAPRESE

MAKES: 2 SERVINGS   **ACTIVE TIME:** 10 MINS   **TOTAL TIME:** 25 MINS

I know it's fall when the weight of our weekly delivery of farm-fresh produce means I can hardly lift the box! Instead of light summer produce like vibrant greens, sweet grapes, and baby potatoes, it's packed to the brim with apples, pears, squash, sweet potatoes, and beets. These substantial fruits and veg give me the kind of nourishment I crave as the temperature starts to dip, and they're perfect for a colder-weather salad. Honeynut and delicata squash (also known as a sweet potato squash) are both sweet and creamy when roasted, have an edible peel, and come in a perfect palm-size portion ideal for a packed lunch. If you're unable to track either down, substitute with peeled butternut squash.

GET AHEAD: Roast the squash for this salad the night before to save time when you are packing your lunch. Or make the whole salad ahead of time and store in the fridge for up to 2 days.

I delicata or 2 small honey nut squash

Olive oil, for drizzling

Salt

4 cups baby arugula or baby spinach

6 oz fresh mozzarella, sliced into ¼-inch slices

2 Tbsp pumpkin seeds

I recipe Creamy Balsamic Dressing (page 114)

1. Preheat the oven to 425°F and line a baking sheet with parchment paper.

2. Slice the squash in half, scoop out and discard the seeds, and slice the squash into ½-inch slices.

3. Place the sliced squash in a medium bowl. Drizzle with olive oil, sprinkle with salt, and toss to coat. Spread out on the prepared baking sheet and roast until cooked through and starting to brown, about 20 minutes. Remove from the oven and set aside to cool.

4. Lay a bed of the arugula in your lunchbox and top with alternating slices of squash and cheese. Sprinkle pumpkin seeds overtop. Pack the dressing on the side and spoon it over the salad before eating.

PACKING TIP: This caprese salad pairs wonderfully with a wedge of crusty baguette.

FARRO NIÇOISE

MAKES: 2 SERVINGS   **ACTIVE TIME:** 5 MINS   **TOTAL TIME:** 15 MINS + COOKING FARRO

Composed salads are a great way to dress up the odds and ends in your fridge, and make for an easy all-in-one meal. While I adore potatoes (a key ingredient in a classic niçoise), some people do not like them at all, so this is for them. In place of potatoes, I use farro, a chewy form of wheat available at Italian markets, health food stores, and many supermarkets.

GET AHEAD: This salad can be made ahead and stored in the fridge for up to 2 days. Or get a jump on it by cooking the farro and storing it in the fridge for up to 1 week. Hard-boiled eggs can also be made in advance and stored in the fridge for up to 1 week.

TARRAGON DRESSING

¼ cup olive oil

1½ Tbsp red wine vinegar

1 tsp Dijon mustard

2 Tbsp packed chopped fresh tarragon, fine stems and leaves only

1 Tbsp sliced green onions, light parts only

⅛ tsp finely minced garlic

Salt and pepper

Small handful green beans, trimmed

1 can olive-oil-packed tuna, drained

3 cups leafy salad greens

2 cups cooked and cooled farro (see Note)

½ cup halved cherry tomatoes

2 hard-boiled eggs, halved

Olives

Quick Pickled Onions (page 178) (optional)

1. Make the dressing: Place the dressing ingredients in a small blender or a tall jar suitable for use with an immersion blender. Blend for about 90 seconds, until combined into a lemon-yellow dressing with tiny flecks of green. Taste and season with salt and pepper as needed (see Note).

2. Place the beans in a microwave-safe dish, cover, and microwave on high for 90 seconds to steam and soften them a little. Break the tuna up into chunks using a fork.

3. Make a bed of the salad greens in your lunch bowl and top with the farro, softened green beans, cherry tomatoes, tuna, hard-boiled eggs, olives, and pickled onions. Pack the dressing in a separate container and toss with the rest of the salad at lunchtime.

PACKING TIP: Add an Apricot Vanilla Muffin (page 195) for a sweet treat to wrap up your meal.

NOTE

Some red wine vinegars can be very acidic; if the dressing catches you at the back of your throat, add ½ to 1 teaspoon granulated sugar and blend again to mollify the acidic flavor. If you can't get your hands on farro, feel free to substitute with quinoa or, of course, some boiled baby potatoes.

SPINACH, ORANGE, & CHICKEN SALAD

MAKES: 2 SERVINGS   **ACTIVE TIME:** 5 MINS   **TOTAL TIME:** 5 MINS + COOKING CHICKEN

One of the highlights of my first job as a teenager was being able to go out and buy my own lunch during my lunch breaks. It felt very grown-up, and I rotated between three spots. One was a big bakery café up the street that had a "sunshine salad" on the menu that I never tired of, and that salad inspired this one. My recipe has a bright and lightly sweetened dressing and a wonderful crunch from the crispy chow mein noodles, just like the original, but I use fresh orange segments instead of the canned ones I enjoyed back then!

GET AHEAD: Plan on using some leftover roast chicken for this recipe, or grilling up some chicken breasts in advance. The salad can be assembled up to 2 days in advance, and stored in the fridge. The dressing can be stored the same way for up to 4 days.

¼ red onion, thinly sliced

6 cups baby spinach

2 cups orange segments

2 cups sliced cooked chicken (rotisserie chicken will do the trick here)

4 Tbsp dried cranberries

4 Tbsp pumpkin seeds

½ cup chow mein noodles (see Note)

LEMON POPPY SEED DRESSING

⅓ cup grapeseed oil

1 Tbsp finely chopped shallots

Juice of 1 lemon

1 Tbsp honey

⅛ tsp salt

1 tsp poppy seeds

1. Soak the red onions in a bowl of ice water for 5 minutes to take the bite out of them, then rinse well.

2. Meanwhile, make the dressing: Put all the dressing ingredients except the poppy seeds into a small blender or a jar suitable for use with an immersion blender. Blend for about 90 seconds, until you have a smooth, light yellow dressing. Add the poppy seeds and stir until dispersed.

3. Make a bed of baby spinach in your lunch bowl and top with the orange segments, red onion slices, chicken, cranberries, and pumpkin seeds. Pack the chow mein noodles and poppy seed dressing on the side, then toss it all together when it's lunchtime.

PACKING TIP: Add a Pear, Vanilla, & Spice Donut (page 204) for a sweet treat to conclude your midday meal.

NOTE

The chow mein noodles in this recipe are the short crispy noodles typically sold in cellophane bags or paper cartons; you should be able to find them in the Chinese or kosher section of the supermarket.

COLD BOWLS

CHICKPEA, ASPARAGUS, & ORZO BOWL

MAKES: 2 SERVINGS   **ACTIVE TIME:** 10 MINS   **TOTAL TIME:** 20 MINS

Orzo is a rice-shaped pasta that is perfect for salads or stirred into soups and stews. I grew up eating it mixed with pesto and wedges of hard-boiled egg on warm summer nights, and I now love it tossed with chickpeas, asparagus, and creamy lemon, dill, and feta dressing. Try to track down a creamy and less salty feta—Persian feta is my absolute favorite—for the best results and texture. This dressing does double duty as a tasty dip for vegetables or tossed with hearty greens.

GET AHEAD: This salad is as delicious the day it is made as it is after a few days in the fridge. The dressing can be made ahead and stored in the fridge for up to 5 days.

1 cup uncooked orzo

2 cups ½-inch-sliced asparagus

1 (15 oz) can chickpeas, drained and rinsed

Olive oil, for drizzling

LEMON, DILL, & FETA DRESSING

1 Tbsp finely chopped shallots

Zest and juice of 1 lemon

½ tsp salt

½ cup coarsely chopped fresh dill

½ cup crumbled feta

½ cup olive oil

2 Tbsp water

1 tsp granulated sugar

Pepper

1. Bring a small pot of salted water to a boil and add the orzo. Cook according to the package instructions—usually about 8 to 9 minutes—until the orzo is al dente.

2. Put the asparagus in the bottom of a colander. When the orzo has cooked, drain it overtop the asparagus to cook the asparagus slightly. Give the colander a shake to drain off the water and tip the orzo and asparagus into a medium bowl. Add the chickpeas and a drizzle of olive oil and stir to coat everything with the oil.

3. Make the dressing: In a small bowl, combine the shallots, lemon zest and juice, and salt and set aside for 5 minutes. While the shallots sit, place the dill, feta, olive oil, water, sugar, and a few grinds of pepper in a small blender or a tall jar suitable for use with an immersion blender. Top with the shallot and lemon mixture. Blend until smooth and emulsified, about 90 seconds.

4. Add about half of the dressing to the bowl with the chickpea mixture and stir to combine. Taste, add more dressing if needed, and season with salt and pepper if needed. Alternatively pack the dressing on the side and toss just before serving.

PACKING TIP: This is a meal in a bowl, so just pack with some fresh fruit for a light conclusion to lunch.

NOTE

Substitute sugar snap peas, frozen peas, or green beans for the asparagus when it is not in season.

NOTE

Tamarind is a pod-like fruit that comes from the tamarind tree. The pulpy fruit and seeds can be purchased in blocks, and as a thick, dark brown concentrate. This recipe calls for the concentrate, which can be found in Indian and Caribbean food shops or health food shops. Be sure not to mix it up with tamarind chutney—although pick up a jar of that too, because it is delicious—and look instead for the plain fruit, which I usually find in small plastic tubs.

FRESH ROLL BOWL

MAKES: 2 SERVINGS   **ACTIVE TIME:** 10 MINS   **TOTAL TIME:** 10 MINS + COOKING PROTEIN

I had my first fresh roll—a bundle of noodles and vegetables wrapped in rice paper—as a teenager in a Vietnamese restaurant, and I have been hooked ever since. I love the combination of fresh fruit, raw vegetables, and fresh herbs and have translated those flavors into this bowl.

GET AHEAD: This bowl can be made ahead and stored in the fridge for up to 2 days; it uses the cooked protein of your choice, so plan to use dinner leftovers. The dressing will keep in the fridge for up to 5 days.

4 oz rice vermicelli

I mango, thinly sliced

I small cucumber, thinly sliced into rounds

I carrot, peeled and grated

I sweet red pepper, diced

½ avocado, diced

8 oz cooked protein (like tofu, grilled chicken, or fish)

I cup mixed chopped fresh herbs (like cilantro, basil, or mint)

I green onion, finely sliced

LIME TAMARIND DRESSING

¼ cup grapeseed oil

I Tbsp honey, or other liquid sweetener

Juice of I lime

2 tsp toasted sesame oil

2 Tbsp finely diced shallots

2 tsp tamarind concentrate (see Note)

1½ tsp tamari

I tsp granulated sugar

Pinch salt

1. Place the vermicelli in a medium bowl and cover with boiling water. Soak according to the package instructions, usually about 3 to 4 minutes, then drain and rinse well. Pack in your lunchbox.

2. Meanwhile, make the dressing: Place the dressing ingredients in a small blender or a tall jar suitable for use with an immersion blender. Blend for about 90 seconds, until the ingredients are combined and you have a smooth, dark brown dressing. Taste and adjust the salt if necessary.

3. Top the noodles with the mango slices, cucumber slices, carrot, red pepper, avocado, and protein. Sprinkle the herbs and green onions overtop. Pack the dressing separately and pour it on immediately before eating.

PACKING TIP: This bowl has everything you need for a full meal midday meal, but you could always pack a little jasmine tea to sip alongside.

GREAT FOR KIDS: Roll the contents of this bowl in rice paper for kids who want to spend more time playing outdoors than lingering over lunch (photo on page 9). Run sheets of rice paper under warm water, lay them out on a plastic cutting board (not a wooden one as the rice paper will stick to it), and top with some noodles, vegetables, and protein. Fold in the sides and then roll up and pack.

SOUTHWESTERN BOWL

MAKES: 2 SERVINGS   **ACTIVE TIME:** 15 MINS   **TOTAL TIME:** 40 MINS

I keep a tube of prepared polenta in my pantry to pull out for a quick dinner, to make crispy polenta fries, or this Southwestern-inspired bowl. Polenta is inexpensive, is relatively easy to find, and has a long shelf life—it's a perfect pantry staple. The dressing I use here is sweet, spicy, and tangy and is a regular in our house. The recipe calls for either sweet smoked paprika or chipotle powder. Chipotle powder is quite spicy and very smoky-tasting, but it can be tricky to track down. Sweet smoked paprika is more readily available and will deliver similar results.

GET AHEAD: The polenta wedges are best the day or day after they are made. The rest of the bowl, including the dressing, can be made ahead and stored in the fridge for up to 3 days.

I small tube (about I lb) prepared polenta

I Tbsp olive oil

Salt

I (15 oz) can black beans, drained and rinsed

I cup corn kernels

I cup sliced cherry tomatoes

½ avocado, diced

¼ cup sliced green onions

CHILI LIME BASIL DRESSING

¼ cup grapeseed oil

¼ cup packed coarsely chopped fresh basil

Juice I lime

I Tbsp honey, or other liquid sweetener

½ tsp sweet smoked paprika or ⅛ tsp chipotle powder

⅛ tsp salt

1. Preheat the oven to 425°F and line a baking sheet with parchment paper.

2. Unwrap the polenta and slice into ½-inch slices. Cut each slice into four wedges and place in a medium bowl. Drizzle the wedges with the olive oil, sprinkle with a big pinch of salt, and gently toss to coat.

3. Tip the wedges onto the prepared baking sheet and roast in the oven for about 25 minutes, until the polenta has deepened in color and the edges have browned. Set aside to cool.

4. Make the dressing: Place the dressing ingredients in a small blender or a jar suitable for use with an immersion blender. Blend for about 90 seconds, until you have a uniform dressing with tiny specks of green basil. Taste and add salt if necessary.

5. Pack the polenta wedges on one side of your lunchbox and add the beans, corn, tomatoes, and avocados next to them. Sprinkle the green onions overtop. Pack a container with the dressing separately from the polenta.

PACKING TIP: This filling bowl has it all, but fresh fruit can be a simple and satisfying addition to any lunch on the go.

NOTE

If the supermarkets and shops around me are any indication, prepared polenta appears to come in large 2-pound-plus tubes or smaller tubes that are about half the size. The smaller (roughly I lb) tubes can typically be found in the natural or organic section of the supermarket. If you find yourself with extra polenta, slice it up into sticks, toss them with some olive oil, scatter some parmesan overtop, and roast in the oven at 425°F until you have crispy polenta fries. Dip the fries in some tomato sauce or serve alongside a piece of grilled fish for dinner.

SESAME NOODLES

MAKES: 2 SERVINGS **ACTIVE TIME:** 10 MINS **TOTAL TIME:** 10 MINS + COOKING NOODLES

I usually keep a small selection of noodles in my pantry so that, with the addition of some fresh or frozen vegetables and protein, I can have a lunch packed or a meal on the table relatively quickly. This recipe calls for udon noodles, a thick and slightly chewy Japanese noodle, but you can substitute with whatever you have in your pantry; it is equally delicious with gluten-free soba or even ramen noodles.

GET AHEAD: This noodle bowl can be made ahead and stored in the fridge for up to 2 days.

SESAME LIME DRESSING

¼ cup tahini

¼ clove garlic, finely chopped or Microplaned

Juice of I lime

I tsp tamari

I tsp granulated sugar

3 Tbsp warm water

⅛ tsp chili oil (optional)

NOODLE BOWL

3 cups cooked udon noodles

2 small cucumbers, sliced into thin rounds

2 carrots, peeled and grated

I cup edamame

¼ cup packed chopped fresh cilantro, both leaves and fine stems

2 Tbsp black sesame seeds

1. Make the dressing: Place the dressing ingredients in a small mixing bowl and whisk to combine until you have a smooth dressing. Tahini will seize when it is initially mixed with citrus, but don't be deterred. Just keep on whisking—it will turn back into a liquid again with some mixing! If you find your dressing is not loosening up enough, add more warm water, a teaspoon at a time, until you achieve a thick but pourable consistency.

2. In a large bowl, toss all of the noodle bowl ingredients together, except the sesame seeds. Pack in lunch containers with the sesame seeds sprinkled over the top, and the dressing on the side. Toss with the dressing just before serving.

PACKING TIP: This lovely light noodle bowl pairs nicely with a selection of sweet, colorful tropical fruits: passionfruit, rambutan, lychee, and dragonfruit are among my favorites.

SUSHI BOWL

MAKES: 2 SERVINGS   **ACTIVE TIME:** 10 MINS   **TOTAL TIME:** 15 MINS + COOKING RICE

All the flavors and components of your favorite maki but without needing the skill to roll it all up! King oyster mushrooms are nearly palm-size and have a very meaty texture when grilled. They are available at Asian supermarkets and at many large grocery stores. This carrot ginger dressing is my take on the vibrant dressing that is served over a pile of iceberg lettuce in sushi spots around Toronto. It is simple and bright and a nice change from traditional vinaigrettes.

GET AHEAD: This bowl, including the dressing, can be made ahead and stored in the fridge for up to 3 days. The recipe calls for cooked rice, which can be made in advance and stored in the fridge for up to 5 days, or freezer for up to 3 months.

4 king oyster mushrooms, halved lengthwise

I green onion, thinly sliced

Toasted sesame oil

Salt

3 cups cooked sushi rice

½ cup sliced cucumbers

½ avocado, sliced or diced

2 carrots, peeled and sliced into ribbons

½ cup edamame

2 radishes, thinly sliced

I small package roasted nori, sliced into strips (see Note)

CARROT GINGER DRESSING

¼ cup grapeseed oil

½ cup grated carrots

I tsp finely chopped ginger

2 Tbsp rice wine vinegar

I tsp diced shallots

½ tsp granulated sugar

⅛ tsp salt

1. Heat a nonstick skillet or grill pan over medium-high heat. In a bowl, toss the oyster mushrooms and green onions with a drizzle of sesame oil and a pinch of salt, then place in the pan. Cook the mushrooms on both sides until browned, about 7 minutes per side. Set aside to cool.

2. Meanwhile, make the dressing: Place the dressing ingredients in a small blender or a jar suitable for use with an immersion blender. Blend for 90 seconds, until you have a uniform, bright orange dressing. Taste and add salt if needed.

3. Pack the rice in your lunchbox. Place the cucumbers, avocados, carrots, edamame, radishes, nori, and cooled mushroom mixture alongside the rice. Pack the dressing separately, topping the bowl with it just before you eat.

PACKING TIP: I used a rice ball maker to make these fun balls of rice shown in the photo. You can find one online or at Japanese shops for under $20; it's a fun gadget to have in your kitchen!

One of our regular sushi spots serves bowls of green tea ice cream at the end of each meal and it hits just the right spot. Ice cream is not terribly practical on the go(!), so I suggest packing a thermal mug of green tea with this sushi, to warm you from the inside out.

NOTE

Packages of toasted nori—delicious sheets of seaweed toasted with sesame oil, salt, and often other toppings—are available in the natural/organic section of supermarkets and at health food stores.

CRISPY TOFU OR CHICKEN BOWL

MAKES: 2 SERVINGS   **ACTIVE TIME:** 15 MINS   **TOTAL TIME:** 35 MINS + COOKING RICE

Crispy cubes of tofu or chicken packed atop some rice and greens is my idea of comfort food! Make the components of this bowl in advance so that you can quickly throw it together in the morning before you head out the door. I usually make a double batch of chicken or tofu and pop it into the fridge for last-minute meals or to satiate what seems like insatiable hunger at the end of the school day.

GET AHEAD: This whole bowl can be made ahead and stored in the fridge for up to 2 days. Or you can get a jump on lunch prep by making extra rice with your dinner one night, and storing it in the fridge for up to 5 days, or in portions in the freezer for up to 3 months. That way you have some on hand to pull out whenever you have a craving for a rice-based bowl. The sauce (see Note) can also be made ahead and stored in the fridge for up to 5 days.

½ block firm tofu, cut into bite-size cubes, or 2 boneless and skinless chicken thighs, cut into bite-size pieces

I egg, lightly beaten or 3 Tbsp dairy-free milk

¼ cup cornstarch mixed with I tsp salt

Cooking spray

8 oz baby bok choy, halved lengthwise

3 cups cooked short-grain rice

I Tbsp sesame seeds

2 green onions, thinly sliced

1. Preheat the oven to 400°F and line a small baking sheet with parchment paper.

2. Dip the tofu cubes or chicken pieces into the beaten egg one at a time, then toss in the cornstarch and salt mixture and place on the baking sheet. Repeat with all the tofu or chicken. Spray generously with cooking spray, then bake for 20 to 25 minutes, until the tofu or chicken has a golden crispy exterior. Set aside to cool.

3. Fill a medium saucepan with salted water and bring to a boil. Add the bok choy and cook for about 3 minutes, until vibrant green and the stalks have softened. Drain well.

4. Meanwhile, make the gochujang sauce: Place the sauce ingredients in a small saucepan and whisk to combine. Heat on medium heat and simmer for 3 to 4 minutes, until the garlic is cooked and the sauce has darkened slightly.

CONTINUES

GOCHUJANG SAUCE

¼ cup gochujang (see Note)

Juice of 1 lime

2 Tbsp toasted sesame oil

1 small clove garlic, finely chopped or Microplaned

1 Tbsp brown sugar

1 Tbsp warm water

5. Pack the rice in the bottom of your lunchbox and top with cooked bok choy and tofu or chicken. Sprinkle the sesame seeds and green onions overtop. Pack the gochujang sauce on the side and drizzle overtop just before eating. This bowl is equally delicious at room temperature or warmed up before serving if you have access to a microwave.

PACKING TIP: This is a hearty bowl that covers nearly all of your bases at lunchtime: protein, veggies, and carbs. Add a side of mixed citrus fruits for a light and bright addition to your lunch.

NOTE

Gochujang is a Korean fermented chili paste made from chilies, rice, fermented soybeans, barley malt powder, and salt. It tastes salty, sweet, and spicy, and once you have tried it, you will be hooked! It is available at some large supermarkets, but it is well worth a visit to a Korean supermarket, where you will have the opportunity to choose between hundreds of different varieties, as well as pick up some other wonderful food. The gochujang sauce can be cooled and stored in an airtight container in the fridge for up to 5 days.

DECONSTRUCTED TACO BOWL

MAKES: 2 SERVINGS   **ACTIVE TIME:** 10 MINS   **TOTAL TIME:** 10 MINS + COOKING RICE

One of my greatest discoveries in the last 10 years has been a little, but wildly popular, Salvadoran restaurant a 20-minute walk from our house. They make the most delicious cheese and chili-stuffed pupusas, and rice and bean tacos, that 75% of my family would happily eat every single day! Tacos on fresh corn tortillas don't pack and travel especially well, but the flavors do. This deconstructed bowl is inspired by the flavors of these tacos and is a wonderful meal to break up the day.

GET AHEAD: This taco bowl *can* be made ahead and stored in the fridge for up to 2 days, but it's best the day it is prepared. Instead, make the rice and store in the fridge for up to 5 days, or freezer for up to 3 months. The dressing (see Note) can also be made ahead and stored in the fridge for up to 3 days.

AVOCADO CILANTRO DRESSING

1 ripe avocado

¼ cup packed coarsely chopped fresh cilantro

1 tsp diced shallots

Juice of 1 lime

⅛ tsp salt

1 to 2 Tbsp water

LIME CREMA

½ cup sour cream or vegan alternative

Juice of ½ lime

¼ tsp salt

1. Make the dressing: Place all the dressing ingredients except the water in a small blender or a jar suitable for use with an immersion blender. Blend for about 90 seconds, until you have a uniform and smooth green dressing. Add 1 tablespoon of water at a time, blending between additions, until the dressing has a consistency similar to Greek yogurt.

2. Make the lime crema: In a small bowl, mix together the sour cream, lime juice, and salt and set aside.

3. Pack the iceberg lettuce in a lunchbox and top with the rice, beans, and cherry tomatoes. Add scoops (this is a scoopable dressing) of the avocado cilantro dressing, drizzle the lime crema overtop, and sprinkle with the queso fresco. Pack the tortilla chips separately from the bowl contents and sprinkle them overtop just before eating.

CONTINUES

3 cups shredded iceberg lettuce

2 cups cooked Spanish-style rice (see Note)

1 (10 oz) can refried beans or an equal amount of kidney beans, drained and rinsed

1 cup halved cherry tomatoes

2 Tbsp crumbled queso fresco, mild feta, or mild vegan cheese

¼ cup crushed plantain or tortilla chips

PACKING TIP: This vibrantly flavored bowl is perfect packed alongside a sliced mango with a squeeze of lime juice and a sprinkle of tajin (a wonderful chili and lime condiment that enhances the sweetness of a ripe mango).

NOTE

This dressing is the perfect recipe for that avocado ripening on the counter that has gone from rock hard to just too soft to dice into a salad. It is runnier and smoother than guacamole but thicker than a traditional salad dressing—perfect for a bowl of grains and vegetables or tossed with hearty greens.

I like to use a Spanish-style rice blend from the grocery store for this bowl. Using pre-seasoned rice adds an additional layer of flavor, as well as a beautiful golden color. Add some cooked shrimp, chicken, or beef to the bowl for extra protein.

WARM BOWLS
(& HANDPIES)

2 IN 1 MEALS

The recipes in this chapter provide you with two ways to enjoy the same basic set of ingredients: one is in a bowl (usually on a bed of pasta, rice, or grain), and the other is folded into some buttery and flaky puff pastry to create handpies. I rely on these "2 for 1" type of recipes during busy weeks when I want to cook just once, and without too much effort, but get both dinner on the table and a jump-start on our lunches for the next day. It's a great time-saving strategy—think and cook once, eat twice—and although my household aren't fans of straightforward, reheated leftovers, once the handpie transformation is complete, they never complain! If you need any more convincing than that, here is my sales pitch for "2 for 1 meals" and handpies overall.

FLEXIBLE QUANTITIES: The recipes in this chapter make enough for two bowls, or four handpies (which are good for four light lunches or two more filling meals). In some cases you may not need to use the full quantity of the recipe for your handpies (it's better to have leftovers to enjoy later than an overstuffed handpie!). Don't hesitate to double or triple these recipes as needed to feed everyone you share the dinner table with, and to have enough to transform into lunches the next day—additionally, many of these recipes freeze beautifully, so you can make an extra big batch and freeze for future use.

PUFF PASTRY FOR ALL SEASONS: I once read that puff pastry was the queen of the kitchen, able to magically transform simple ingredients into something much more delicious, and I completely agree (and hope once you've tried these recipes that you will too!). I always keep a box in my freezer, and use it to fold around leftovers for lunch, or bacon and cheese for brunch (page 26), or some ripe fruit for a sweet handpie treat (page 210). The puff pastry I normally buy comes in a 1 lb box with two separately sealed sheets, usually 10- or 12-inch squares of pastry each, rolled up and individually frozen. You can use either size of pastry square interchangeably. Look for puff pastry made with butter for the best flavor; however, if you prefer to avoid dairy, check out the kosher section of a large supermarket for puff pastry that is marked "parve" on the packaging—this means it will not contain any dairy products.

No time to make the fillings in this chapter but still feel like a handpie? Improvise with what you have in your fridge or pantry: puff pastry baked around feta, brie or other soft cheeses, with some added jam or pesto (including the recipes on pages 184 to 188), is seriously delicious!

PUFF PASTRY FOR ALL EPICUREANS: Puff pastry is a great kitchen equalizer, easy for both the novice and experienced food lover to work with; once thawed, you simply need to unroll it and cut it out. Feeling uncertain about freestyling? Pick up a pastry press, a hinged tool that not only cuts out perfect circles of dough but also closes up and crimps the edges together. They are under $15 and one of the few single purpose kitchen tools I'm a fan of.

GREAT FOR KIDS: Little hands love little handpies baked into lovely little shapes. Instead of making the larger rectangular pies described on the next page, try using cookie cutters to make small circular, heart-shaped, or even square pies for your kids using cookie cutters. Reduce the baking time by about 3 minutes, depending on the size of the handpies you create.

EVEN THE SCRAPS ARE DELICIOUS: Don't despair over the scraps of dough leftover from cutting out cute shapes. I cut them into bite-size pieces, brush them with egg, and sprinkle them generously with sharp shredded cheese and then a pinch of sweet smoked paprika (or just cinnamon sugar for a sweet option), and bake them on a parchment-lined baking sheet at the same time as the handpies. They make a great snack—quickly gobbled up as soon as they come out of the oven (if my family is any indication!).

HANDPIES 101

MAKES: 4 HANDPIES (SERVES 2 FOR A FILLING MEAL, OR 4 FOR A LIGHT LUNCH)
ACTIVE TIME: 10 MINUTES + FILLING PREP **TOTAL TIME:** 30 MINUTES + FILLING PREP

The Queen of the Kitchen (aka puff pastry) is available in the freezer section of your supermarket and needs to be thawed in the fridge overnight before use. Warm puff pastry is difficult to work with—it gets sticky and frustrating to manipulate—so be sure to pull it out of the fridge just before use (and pop it back into the fridge or freezer for a few minutes to cool down if it's sticking to itself). To make vegan handpies, use kosher puff pastry—it will not have any butter—and substitute either a vegan egg replacement or some dairy-free milk for the eggs called for in the recipe. You won't get quite the same shine on your pies, but they'll still taste delicious.

GET AHEAD: Handpies are definitely best the day they are baked, but you *can* prebake (and crisp them up again later) if you want to. Here are a couple of options for doing the heavy lifting ahead of time:

- **PREPARE BUT DO NOT BAKE (THIS IS WHAT I'D RECOMMEND):** store in the fridge for up to 12 hours, or freezer for up to 3 months. To prevent unbaked handpies from sticking together in the freezer, freeze them first on a parchment-lined baking sheet; when frozen solid, transfer to an airtight container or freezer bag. Bake unbaked frozen handpies on a parchment-lined baking sheet at 425°F for 20 minutes.

- **PREBAKE:** store, tightly wrapped in foil, in the fridge for up to 2 days. Crisp up your prebaked pies for 10 minutes at 200°F, if you can, before enjoying for lunch.

1 sheet puff pastry, thawed but still cool

1 recipe handpie filling (pages 26, and 153 to 171)

1 egg, lightly beaten

1. Preheat the oven to 400°F and line a baking sheet with parchment paper. On a lightly floured surface, unroll the puff pastry sheet. Using a sharp knife or pastry cutter, cut it into quarters so that you have four squares, and then cut each square into a set of two rectangles. One rectangle will be the bottom of each hand pie and the other one will serve as the top.

CONTINUES

2. Scoop one-quarter of the filling mixture onto each of the bottom rectangles and spread it out evenly using the back of a spoon or a small offset spatula, leaving a ¼-inch border around all edges.

3. Using the point of a sharp knife, cut a few small vents in each of the top rectangles to allow steam to escape while baking. Feel free to get creative with the style of the vents!

4. Using a pastry brush, paint the ¼-inch border of the bottom rectangles with a little of the beaten egg. Carefully top each filled bottom rectangle with its corresponding top rectangle "lid." Use your fingers or a fork to gently press down and seal all the edges. Transfer the pies to the prepared baking sheet and brush the tops generously with the remaining beaten egg.

5. Bake for 20 minutes (or at 425°F for 20 minutes if baking from frozen), until puffed up and golden brown (the pies will be crispy, and you'll see the lovely layers of pastry have puffed up along the edges). Allow the handpies to cool before packing as the pastry will get soggy if it is packed while still warm.

PACKING TIP: Rich and savory handpies pair well with fresh and light green salads or raw vegetables. Add a container of preserved-lemon dressing (like the dressing from the Roasted Cauliflower, Manouri, & Pomegranate Salad, page 107) or try the Tarragon Dressing (page 122), to drizzle over your salad for a punch of flavor.

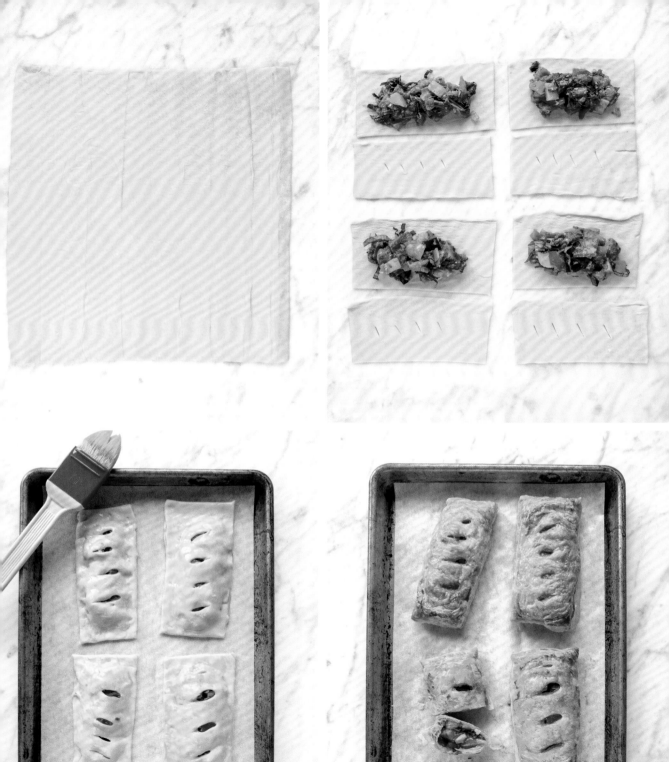

BROTHY BEANS & GREENS BOWL

MAKES: 2 BOWLS OR 4 HANDPIES   **ACTIVE TIME:** 15 MINS   **TOTAL TIME:** 15 MINS

We eat probably more than our fair share of dark leafy greens thanks to the farm box that arrives on our doorstep each week. At some point every few months, my family has had their fill of raw kale salads (see page 113) or of my favorite Deep Green Fall Pesto (see page 184), so I take our weekly bunch of kale and make a bowl of beans and greens in a garlic and shallot-infused broth. It is simple, delicious, and the perfect warm bowl for a fall day. It can be a tough sell to my family, though, so I pack it into some puff pastry to their—and really my—delight.

GET AHEAD: This bowl can be made up to 2 days ahead of time and stored in the fridge.

2 Tbsp olive oil

Pinch chili flakes

¼ cup finely diced shallots

2 cloves garlic, thinly sliced

1 bunch kale, leaves only, chopped

1 cup canned butter beans, drained and rinsed

½ cup vegetable or chicken stock

½ lemon

¼ cup packed finely grated parmesan or vegan parmesan

Salt and pepper

BOWLS

2 cups vegetable or chicken stock

HANDPIES

1 recipe Handpies 101 (page 149)

1. In a medium skillet over medium heat, warm the olive oil. Add the chili flakes and shallots and cook for 3 minutes, giving the pan a shake every so often. Add the garlic slices and cook for another minute. Add the kale and cook until it has wilted, about 3 minutes.

2. Add the beans, pour in the stock, and simmer until all the liquid has evaporated, about 3 minutes. Add a squeeze of lemon juice, fold in the parmesan, and add a few grinds of pepper. Have a taste and add some salt if needed.

3. BOWLS: Add the stock and toss everything in the pan together to warm through. Serve warm (see Packing Tip below).

4. HANDPIES: Let the filling cool down as you prepare the pastry and set things up to bake. Turn to page 150 for filling, wrapping, baking, and packing directions.

PACKING TIP: Pack the hot brothy beans and greens in a pre-warmed thermos (see page 22) or in a microwavable container to warm up at lunchtime. Add an extra container of grated parmesan to top them with, just before serving, and a wedge of baguette for soaking up the broth.

CURRIED SWEET POTATOES, CHICKPEAS, & SPINACH BOWL

MAKES: 2 BOWLS OR 4 HANDPIES   **ACTIVE TIME:** 20 MINS   **TOTAL TIME:** 35 MINS

I adore the combination of sweet potato and warm spices like cumin, coriander, fennel, and tur-meric. This curry has all of those, thanks to one of my favorite pantry staples: curry paste. Then I've added some chickpeas and spinach, some lime to liven things up, and a splash of cream. Enjoy this warm over a bowl of rice or folded into some puff pastry for a curry on the go.

GET AHEAD: This curry improves with age, and will be even better the day after you make it. Get a jump on your lunch prep by making it up to 3 days in advance, then storing in the fridge. The rice can also be made in advance, and stored in the fridge for up to 5 days, or freezer for up to 3 months.

1 Tbsp grapeseed oil

1 Tbsp yellow curry paste

¼ cup ¼-inch-diced onions

1½ cups peeled and ¼-inch-diced sweet potatoes

Salt

3 Tbsp water

¾ cup chickpeas

2 handfuls baby spinach

Juice of 1 lime

1 Tbsp heavy cream

BOWLS

¼ cup heavy cream, or coconut milk

3 cups cooked rice, for packing

HANDPIES

1 recipe Handpies 101 (page 149)

1. In a medium saucepan over medium-high heat, warm the oil. Add the curry paste and cook for about 1 minute, stirring constantly. Add the onions and cook for about 2 minutes.

2. Add the sweet potatoes, a big pinch of salt, and the water. Lower the heat, cover the pot, and cook until the sweet potatoes have softened but still hold their shape, about 12 to 15 minutes. Add the chickpeas, baby spinach, and lime juice and stir to combine. Stir in the cream and have a taste. Add more salt if needed.

3. BOWLS: Add the extra ¼ cup cream to the pan and a splash of water if the curry seems a bit dry. Toss in the pan to combine. Serve warm, with the rice (see Packing Tip below).

4. HANDPIES: Let the filling cool down as you prepare the pastry and set things up to bake. Turn to page 150 for filling, wrapping, baking, and packing directions.

PACKING TIP: Pack this warming curry in a thermos or microwavable container on a bed of rice. A simple side of mango, or other sweet fresh fruit, is a light end to a perfect cold-weather meal.

NOTE

Substitute coconut milk for the cream to make this curry vegan.

MOROCCAN SPICE STEW

MAKES: 2 BOWLS OR 4 HANDPIES   **ACTIVE TIME:** 20 MINS   **TOTAL TIME:** 35 MINS

One of the last meals my husband and I had before the world shut down in 2020 was on a chilly evening at a little neighborhood pub. We were running to catch a movie that evening and just wanted to grab a quick bite, and we were pleasantly surprised at how lovely our food was. I had a wonderful Moroccan-style tagine that hit the spot—and I've had plenty of time to master recreating it at home since! My version of this dish comes together with some pantry and refrigerator staples and a pinch of Moroccan spice mix.

GET AHEAD: This stew comes together quickly but also improves with a night in the fridge, so don't hesitate to make it in advance and warm it up before heading out the door for the day. It can be stored in an airtight container in the fridge for up to 5 days, or freezer for up to 3 months. Like soup, divide and freeze in portions so you can grab only what you need.

I Tbsp olive oil

¼ cup ¼-inch-diced onions

¼ to ½ tsp Moroccan spice mix (see Note)

I cup peeled and ¼-inch-diced butternut squash

¼ cup peeled and ¼-inch-diced carrots

½ cup canned chickpeas, drained and rinsed

Salt

½ cup store-bought tomato sauce

¼ cup quartered dried apricots

Big handful baby spinach

½ lime

1. In a medium saucepan over medium-high heat, heat the oil. Add the onions and spice mix and cook for 2 minutes while stirring. Add the squash, carrots, chickpeas, and a big pinch of salt and cook for about 3 minutes, until the onions are translucent.

2. Add the tomato sauce and apricots. Cover the pan, reduce the heat to medium-low, and cook until the squash has softened, about 10 to 15 minutes. Stir in the spinach and a big squeeze of lime juice. Taste and adjust the seasoning if required.

3. BOWLS: Add the additional tomato sauce, water, and dried apricots. Simmer for a minute to combine. Serve warm with the couscous (see Packing Tip on page 158).

4. HANDPIES: Let the filling cool down as you prepare the pastry and set things up to bake. Turn to page 150 for filling, wrapping, baking, and packing directions, making sure to sprinkle the handpies with nigella seeds, if using, before they go in the oven.

CONTINUES

½ cup store-bought tomato
   sauce

½ cup water

¼ cup quartered dried
   apricots

3 cups cooked couscous

HANDPIES

1 recipe Handpies 101
   (page 149)

Nigella seeds (optional)

PACKING TIP: Pack the stew in a pre-warmed thermos (see page 22) or microwavable container on top of a bed of couscous. This wonderful spiced and slightly spicy stew pairs well with some cooling yogurt. Pack yourself a small container of plain Greek yogurt topped with a sprinkle of the spice mix, a drizzle of olive oil and a handful of fresh cilantro leaves. Top the stew with the yogurt before serving.

NOTE

There is no need to make a special trip to find a Moroccan spice blend! One of my favorite blends is from a massive multinational corporation and is a blend of chilies, cayenne, coriander, cumin, caraway seeds, fennel, garlic, and more. It is sold in little packages in the spice section of every supermarket I have visited, and is a great addition to this stew as well as to soups and other dishes.

MUSHROOM STROGANOFF

MAKES: 2 BOWLS OR 4 HANDPIES   **ACTIVE TIME:** 20 MINS   **TOTAL TIME:** 30 MINS

I had mushroom stroganoff for the first time at a restaurant overlooking the Baltic Sea in Tallinn, Estonia, a few years ago. We ended up at the restaurant solely because it shares a name with our eldest daughter, but in the end, we enjoyed a meal of updated Russian classics. Stroganoff is traditionally made with beef—this one uses beefy mini portobello mushrooms instead—in a sour cream–enhanced sauce. Enjoy it hot with egg noodles or fold it into puff pastry for a delicious midday meal.

GET AHEAD: Make the egg noodles and mushroom mixture in advance and store in the fridge for up to 5 days (noodles) and 3 days (mushrooms); have a quick taste when you warm them up for lunch and adjust the seasoning as needed. Alternatively, if multitasking in the morning, boil the noodles at the same time as you cook the mushrooms.

3 Tbsp butter

I onion, ¼-inch-diced

2 cloves garlic, thinly sliced

4 cups thinly sliced mini portobello or cremini mushrooms

4 tsp white wine vinegar

I Tbsp all-purpose flour

½ cup vegetable or chicken stock

2 Tbsp sour cream

¼ cup packed chopped fresh parsley, leaves and fine stems

I green onion, thinly sliced

Salt and pepper

1. In a medium skillet over medium heat, melt 2 tablespoons of the butter. Add the onions and garlic and sauté, stirring occasionally, for about 5 minutes, until the onions are translucent. Add the mushrooms and cook for 10 minutes, until they have released their moisture and started to brown. Stir in the vinegar. Use the spoon to scrape up any brown bits on the bottom of the pan. Remove from heat and set aside while you make the sauce.

2. In a small saucepan over medium heat, add the remaining 1 tablespoon of butter and the flour and cook, stirring continuously, until the mixture is golden. Pour in the stock and cook, stirring, until it has thickened, about 2 minutes. Turn off the heat and stir in the sour cream, parsley, and green onions. Pour the sauce over the mushrooms and stir to combine. Taste and add salt and pepper as needed.

CONTINUES

BOWLS

½ cup vegetable or chicken
   stock

3 cups cooked egg noodles

Green onion and chives,
   chopped, for garnish

HANDPIES

1 recipe Handpies 101
   (page 149)

3. BOWLS: Add the extra ½ cup stock to the pan and stir to combine with the mushrooms. Serve warm with the mushrooms on top of the noodles, or tossed to combine if you prefer (see Packing Tip below). Garnish with green onion and chives.

4. HANDPIES: Let the filling cool down as you prepare the pastry and set things up to bake. Turn to page 150 for filling, wrapping, baking, and packing directions.

PACKING TIP: Pack the stroganoff and noodles in a pre-warmed thermos (see page 22) or microwavable container. This stick-to-your-ribs warm lunch would pair well with a light and easy leafy green salad. Top the salad with a simple bright dressing—the Basil & Mint Dressing on page 103 would be perfect.

NOTE

Cut the mushrooms into bite-size pieces if you are making bowls, and into a small dice (about ¼ inch) for handpies.

DUMPLING NOODLE BOWL

MAKES: 2 BOWLS OR 4 HANDPIES   **ACTIVE TIME:** 20 MINS   **TOTAL TIME:** 20 MINS

We have been regulars at a dumpling restaurant in Toronto's downtown Chinatown from the time it was a tiny warren of rooms in a funny split-level building that was eventually replaced by condos. By the time our daughters were born, it had relocated to a bigger space where we could all watch in awe as dough was made, rolled out, filled, and intricately folded into our favorite dumplings. This recipe is inspired by the flavors of those dumplings. If you feel inclined, pick up a package of dumpling wrappers and use this mix to make your own dumplings.

GET AHEAD: Make the mushroom and tofu mixture up to 2 days ahead and store in the fridge. Cook the noodles as close to the time you plan to eat them, to keep them fresh.

1 Tbsp toasted sesame oil

2 tsp finely minced garlic

2 tsp finely minced ginger

3 cups chopped mushrooms (a mix of enoki, king oyster, shiitake, or whatever is available) (see Note)

2 stalks celery, ¼-inch-diced

½ block extra-firm tofu, cubed

3 green onions, thinly sliced

1 Tbsp tamari

1 tsp rice wine vinegar

Salt

BOWLS

2 cups cooked noodles (like soba, rice or udon)

HANDPIES

1 recipe Handpies 101 (page 149)

1. In a skillet over medium-high heat, warm the sesame oil. Add the garlic and ginger and cook for about a minute, stirring constantly, until fragrant. Add the mushrooms and cook for 5 to 6 minutes, stirring every so often. Add the celery, tofu, and green onions and cook until the mixture in the pan is dry, about 5 minutes. Stir in the tamari and rice wine vinegar, allow it to cook for a minute, then turn off the heat. Taste and season with salt if needed.

2. BOWLS: Cook your noodles at the last minute (freshly cooked noodles are always better than ones that have been sitting in the fridge). Serve the noodles warm topped with the mushroom and tofu mixture (see Packing Tip below).

3. HANDPIES: Let the filling cool down as you prepare the pastry and set things up to bake. Transfer the cooled filling to a food processor fitted with the steel blade, and pulse for 10 to 15 seconds until finely chopped. Turn to page 150 for filling, wrapping, baking, and packing directions.

PACKING TIP: Pack the tofu and mushroom mixture and the noodles in a pre-warmed thermos (see page 22) or microwavable container. This bowl is mild and mellow so I pair it with something bright and crispy: Pack it with some slaw (like the one on page 61) for a complementary burst of flavor.

FRENCH ONION SOUP PASTA

MAKES: 2 BOWLS OR 4 HANDPIES   **ACTIVE TIME:** 20 MINS   **TOTAL TIME:** 25 MINS

I invariably come home from the supermarket with a bag of onions only to find that we already have two bags in the pantry, or I skip the onion aisle entirely because I am sure we have lots at home only to discover when I get back that there are none at all. This recipe takes care of two onions, for those times you find yourself with an abundance, and captures the essence of a bowl of French onion soup.

GET AHEAD: Kitchen multitasking is my favorite kind of multitasking! Put a pot of water on to boil and cook your pasta while you are making the onions. Or, you can make both the pasta and the onion mixture in advance, and store in the fridge for up to 5 days (pasta) and 3 days (onions), then just throw everything into a pan in the morning to quickly heat up.

1 Tbsp butter

2 medium onions, thinly sliced

1 Tbsp chopped fresh sage

1 clove garlic, thinly sliced

2 Tbsp white balsamic
  vinegar

Salt and pepper

BOWLS

1 cup grated gruyère plus
  more for serving

3 cups cooked pasta

1 cup chickpeas

HANDPIES

1 cup grated gruyère

1 recipe Handpies 101
  (page 149)

1. In a skillet over medium heat, melt the butter. Add the sliced onions and sage and cook for 7 to 8 minutes, stirring occasionally, until the onions have softened and started to brown. Add the sliced garlic and cook for 2 more minutes, stirring, until the garlic is fragrant and cooked through. Add the vinegar—it will bubble enthusiastically—and stir to scrape up any brown bits on the bottom of the pan. Add a big pinch of salt and a few grinds of pepper.

2. BOWLS: Add the cheese, pasta, and chickpeas to the pan and toss to combine. Add a splash of water if your pasta looks a bit fry. Serve warm (see Packing Tip), topped with more grated cheese just before serving.

3. HANDPIES: Let the onions cool down, then stir in the cheese. Let the filling cool down as you prepare the pastry and set things up to bake. Turn to page 150 for filling, wrapping, baking, and packing directions.

PACKING TIP: Pack the pasta in a pre-warmed thermos (see page 22) or microwavable container to be heated at lunchtime. This rich and unctuous warm meal is perfect paired with a light green salad dressed with a simple vinaigrette (like the White Balsamic & Parmesan Dressing on page 113).

NOTE

Unlike traditional ratatouille, this recipe calls for Japanese eggplant. Japanese eggplant is usually sweeter and doesn't require salting to remove any bitterness. If you can't find one at your supermarket, substitute the same amount of regular eggplant, but do your best to use the smallest ones you can find (they tend to be much less bitter and don't require salting).

RATATOUILLE BOWL

MAKES: 2 BOWLS OR 4 HANDPIES   **ACTIVE TIME:** 15 MINS   **TOTAL TIME:** 15 MINS

If you receive seasonal produce deliveries to your home, or are an avid home gardener, you probably find yourself, as I invariably do, with armfuls of zucchini, eggplant, tomatoes, and peppers every summer. Ratatouille, the magical dish from Provence, is my favorite way to put these vegetables to good use. This recipe, thanks to the inclusion of the Sundried Tomato Pesto (page 185), comes together quickly to create a flavorful and satisfying meal.

GET AHEAD: This recipe calls for Sundried Tomato Pesto (page 185), which can be made ahead and stored in the fridge for up to 1 week, or freezer for up to 3 months. The ratatouille can be made ahead and stored in the fridge for up to 3 days.

2 Tbsp olive oil

2 cloves garlic, finely minced

Pinch chili flakes

1 cup finely diced sweet yellow or red onion

1½ cups ¼-inch-diced zucchini or summer squash

1½ cups ¼-inch-diced Japanese eggplant (see Note)

1½ cups ¼-inch-diced sweet pepper

½ cup Sundried Tomato Pesto (page 185)

¼ cup chopped fresh basil

Salt and pepper

BOWLS

1 cup vegetable stock

3 cups cooked long-grain rice (like basmati)

HANDPIES

1 recipe Handpies 101 (page 149)

1. In a medium skillet over medium heat, warm the olive oil. Add the garlic and chili flakes and cook, stirring regularly, until fragrant, about 1 minute. Add the onion and cook, stirring regularly, until the onion is translucent, about 3 to 4 minutes. Add the zucchini, eggplant, and pepper and cook, stirring occasionally, until they have softened, about 5 to 8 minutes. Turn off the heat and stir in the pesto and basil. Taste and season with salt and pepper if needed.

2. BOWLS: Add the stock to the skillet and stir into the vegetable mixture. Have a quick taste to check the seasoning. Serve the ratatouille with the rice (see Packing Tip below).

3. HANDPIES: Let the filling cool down as you prepare the pastry and set things up to bake. Turn to page 150 for filling, wrapping, baking, and packing directions.

PACKING TIP: Ratatouille is one of those rare dishes that is lovely to eat at all temperatures. Pack it with the rice in a pre-warmed thermos (see page 22), or in a microwavable bowl. Alternatively, pack it cold, and allow it to warm up to room temperature before enjoying. Ratatouille is also delicious served with some crusty baguette to soak up all of the delectable juices from the vegetables.

CHICKEN POT PIE STEW

MAKES: 2 BOWLS OR 4 HANDPIES   **ACTIVE TIME:** 20 MINS   **TOTAL TIME:** 35 MINS

If you find yourself with a cup of cooked chicken and a collection of ordinary fresh or frozen vegetables but without a plan, this is the recipe for you. Chicken pot pie stew—either in a bowl or baked into some puff pastry—transforms that chicken and veg into a nostalgic dish perfect for your lunchbox.

GET AHEAD: This stew can be made up to 2 days in advance, and stored in the fridge. Heat it up just before you head out the door. The recipe calls for cooked chicken: make it in advance, or plan for some leftovers, or use supermarket rotisserie chicken.

I Tbsp olive oil

¼ cup ¼-inch-diced onions

¼ cup ¼-inch-diced potatoes

¼ cup ¼-inch-diced carrots

¼ cup ¼-inch-diced celery

I cup chicken stock

I Tbsp fresh thyme leaves

I tsp cornstarch

I cup cooked and cubed (or shredded) chicken

2 Tbsp corn kernels

2 Tbsp peas

Salt and pepper

BOWLS

I cup chicken stock

Splash of milk

Squeeze of lemon juice

HANDPIES

I recipe Handpies IOI (page I49)

1. In a medium saucepan over medium-high heat, warm the olive oil. Add the onions, potatoes, carrots, and celery and cook for 5 minutes, stirring occasionally. Add the chicken stock and thyme leaves. Bring to a simmer, cover, and cook until the potatoes are cooked through but still maintain their shape, about 15 minutes.

2. Add the cornstarch and bring to a gentle boil to thicken the mixture. Stir in the chicken, corn, and peas as well as a few grinds of pepper. Taste and season with salt if needed.

3. BOWLS: Add another cup of stock to the pan, a splash of milk, and a squeeze of lemon juice. Toss in the pan to combine and adjust the seasoning if necessary. Serve warm (see Packing Tip below).

4. HANDPIES: Let the filling cool down as you prepare the pastry and set things up to bake. Turn to page 150 for filling, wrapping, baking, and packing directions.

PACKING TIP: Pack this hearty chicken pot pie stew hot in a pre-warmed thermos (see page 22) or in a microwavable container to warm up at lunchtime. Tuck a store-bought biscuit or scone in with the stew for a truly satisfying cold-weather meal.

NOTE

Look out for tubes of tomato paste at the supermarket, as these allow you to squeeze out only as much as you need for a recipe. I usually pick up half a dozen tubes whenever I visit Italian markets and pop them into my pantry to use for soups and stews. If you can only get your hands on small cans of tomato paste, freeze what is leftover in an airtight container for up to 3 months.

QUICK SPAGHETTI BOLOGNESE

MAKES: 2 BOWLS OR 4 HANDPIES   **ACTIVE TIME:** 20 MINS   **TOTAL TIME:** 20 MINS

This is not your nonna's meat sauce, but it is a rich and delicious sauce perfect for a bowl of spaghetti or for filling a handpie. It's a lunch-hour crowd pleaser, made even better by the fact that it freezes beautifully, so you can make it in advance, freeze it in portions, and then just pull out of the freezer what you need to warm up and pack for lunch! Don't hesitate to double this recipe and keep a stash of sauce on hand for a busy weeknight meal.

GET AHEAD: Make this sauce in advance and store in the fridge for up to 5 days, or the freezer for up to 3 months. This recipe calls for cooked pasta; for best results, cook it while you are making the sauce and toss everything together in the pan before packing.

½ lb ground chuck

½ cup ¼-inch-diced onions

½ cup ¼-inch-diced carrots

½ cup ¼-inch-diced celery

2 cloves garlic, thinly sliced

3 Tbsp tomato paste (see Note)

2 Tbsp heavy cream

Salt and pepper

BOWLS

1½ cups store-bought tomato sauce

3 cups cooked spaghetti

2 Tbsp grated parmesan

Fresh basil leaves, for garnish

HANDPIES

1 recipe Handpies 101 (page 149)

1. Warm a skillet over medium-high heat, then add the ground chuck. Cook, stirring often, until browned, about 5 minutes. Pour off most of the fat, then add the onions, carrots, celery, and garlic and cook until they have softened, about 5 minutes. Add the tomato paste and cook for 3 minutes, until it has darkened. Stir in the cream and add a big pinch of salt and a few grinds of pepper. Taste and adjust the seasoning if necessary.

2. BOWLS: Add the tomato sauce to the pan and stir to combine. Serve warm with the sauce on top of the spaghetti, or tossed to combine (see Packing Tip below). Top with the parmesan and basil just before serving.

3. HANDPIES: Let the filling cool down as you prepare the pastry and set things up to bake. Turn to page 150 for filling, wrapping, baking, and packing directions.

PACKING TIP: Pack this simple but hearty pasta bowl hot in a pre-warmed thermos (see page 22) or microwavable container to heat at lunchtime, along with a container of simple, sweet fresh grapes for a light and bright accompaniment.

p. 175

p. 176

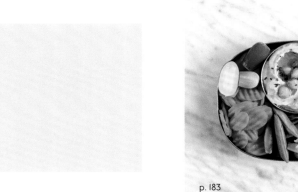
p. 183

p. 186

SNACKS, DIPS, & SPREADS

PUFF PASTRY CHEESE STICKS

MAKES: 24 STICKS   **ACTIVE TIME:** 10 MINS   **TOTAL TIME:** 35 MINS

Cheese sticks are a great snack on their own, with a handful of grapes or an apple, or with other tasty nibbles like charcuterie, cheese, and more. Make them with whatever sharp hard cheese you have on hand—I usually use odds and ends that are hanging about in our cheese drawer—and feel free to play around with different combinations.

GET AHEAD: These cheese sticks can be made ahead and stored at room temperature for up to I week, or in the freezer for up to I month.

1 sheet puff pastry, thawed (see Note)

1 egg, lightly beaten

1½ cups shredded sharp hard cheese (cheddar, gruyère, comté, etc.)

Sweet smoked paprika

Salt and pepper

NOTE

Puff pastry is available in the freezer section of your supermarket. See Handpies 101 (page 149) for more info, tips, and tricks for working with puff pastry.

1. Preheat the oven to 400°F and line a baking sheet with parchment paper.

2. Unroll your puff pastry onto the baking sheet. Using a pastry brush, brush the surface of the pastry with some of the egg. Evenly sprinkle the cheese overtop, followed by a few pinches of paprika, a pinch of salt, and a couple of good grinds of pepper.

3. Using a pastry cutter or sharp knife, slice the square of pastry into two so that you have two rectangles. Cut each of the rectangles into about 12 x 1-inch-wide strips. Distribute the sticks over the baking sheet, twisting each one with a corkscrewing motion a couple of times as you go. Dab any exposed pastry with a bit more of the beaten egg and top with any cheese that fell off the cheese sticks when you moved them on the baking sheet.

4. Bake in the oven for 15 to 20 minutes, until puffed up and golden brown. Transfer to a cooling rack and allow to fully cool before transferring to an airtight container for storage.

PACKING TIP: Pack these cheese sticks alongside a thermos of hot soup for lunch, or in a snackbox with vegetables and dip, like Cannellini, Lemon, & Basil Dip (page 181), or just on their own for a savory bite to eat when you're feeling peckish.

BAGEL CHIPS

MAKES: ABOUT 8 CHIPS PER BAGEL **ACTIVE TIME:** 5 MINS **TOTAL TIME:** 20 MINS

Never waste another bagel! I usually buy bagels by the dozen and invariably end up with two or three that are a bit too stale to eat but that I hate to waste. Instead of tossing them in the compost, I slice them up thinly, toss them with a drizzle of olive oil, and bake them until they are crispy. The resulting bagel chips are perfect for scooping up dips or for eating as a quick snack on their own.

GET AHEAD: These bagel chips can be made ahead and stored at room temperature for up to 1 week.

Bagel(s)

Olive oil, for drizzling

Salt

NOTE

The number of chips will vary depending on the kind and size of bagels you use. Montreal-style bagels are our favorite and are more hole than dough so the yield here is on the smaller side. Expect more chips if you are using a doughier bagel. We usually buy everything or salted poppy seed bagels, so I salt sparingly. If you are using bagels that are not already salted, you may want to add a bit more salt.

1. Preheat the oven to 350°F and line a baking sheet with parchment paper.

2. Place a bagel flat on a cutting board. Using a bread knife, slice (downwards, not across) into roughly ⅛- to ¼-inch slices. Depending on your bagel, you will end up with a collection of oblongs or a mix of oblongs and circles if your bagel has a big hole in the middle! Repeat if using more than one bagel.

3. Put your bagel slices into a large bowl and drizzle them with olive oil—use 1 tablespoon oil for every bagel you started with. Add a sprinkle of salt as desired (see Note). Using your hands or a rubber spatula, toss everything together until the bagel slices are evenly coated with olive oil.

4. Tip the slices out of the bowl onto the parchment-lined baking sheet and spread them out evenly. Bake for 10 to 15 minutes, until the slices are medium brown. Allow to cool completely before packing.

PACKING TIP: Pack these crunchy bagel chips with some Smoky Black Bean Dip (page 180) and raw veggies for a delicious midmorning or midafternoon snack. Or alongside a thermos of soup for dipping.

QUICK PICKLED ONIONS

MAKES: 1 CUP   **ACTIVE TIME:** 2 MINS   **TOTAL TIME:** 20 MINS

Pickled onions are truly one of the easiest things to make and add a huge punch of flavor to a salad, sandwich, burger, grain bowl, or even a slice of pizza. I always keep a jar in my fridge and count on them to add some oomph to those dishes that are missing a certain something.

GET AHEAD: These onions come together so quickly you can make them the morning of, but having some on hand is always a time-saver. Store (preferably in a glass container), in the fridge for up to 10 days.

½ red onion, thinly sliced

¼ cup vinegar (like rice wine, cider, or white wine vinegar)

1 tsp granulated sugar

1 tsp salt

1 tsp whole peppercorns

1 tsp your favorite spices (like caraway, cumin, fennel seeds, or chili flakes) (optional)

1. Place the red onion in a glass measuring cup or jug. Top with the vinegar, sugar, salt, peppercorns, and any additional whole spices you would like to add. Stir to dissolve the sugar and salt. Add enough water to the measuring cup to fully cover the onions by about half an inch.

2. Cover the measuring cup with a lid or microwave-safe plastic wrap, and microwave on high for 3 minutes. Set aside to cool before transferring to an airtight glass container and storing in the fridge.

PACKING TIP: Pickled onions are called for in the Vibrant Quinoa Salad (page 104) and the Farro Niçoise (page 122).

CRISPY CANNELLINI BEANS

MAKES: ABOUT 2 CUPS   **ACTIVE TIME:** 10 MINS   **TOTAL TIME:** 25 MINS

Crispy cannellini beans were a bit of a kitchen epiphany one evening when I was making dinner and did not have any bread to whip up some croutons. I looked to my pantry for a solution, and there was a can of beans sitting front and center. I decided to throw them in a pan with some olive oil and was delighted with the outcome, as were my family. They are a staple in our house now, and we all enjoy nibbling on them out of a bowl or tossed with some hearty salad greens.

GET AHEAD: These beans can be made ahead and stored in the fridge for up to 4 days.

I (15 oz) can cannellini beans, drained and dried (see Note)

2 Tbsp olive oil

I sprig rosemary, leaves only

Salt and pepper

Lemon wedge

NOTE

The beans will cook more quickly and be crispier if they are dried before being tipped into a pan. If my oven is already on, I tip the beans onto a baking sheet and pop them in the oven to dry for about 10 minutes, giving them a shake midway. If your oven is not on, spread the drained beans out onto a clean kitchen towel and allow them to dry off.

Photo on page 113

1. In a large skillet over medium-high heat, heat the olive oil. When the oil is hot, add the rosemary and beans and cook, tossing every few minutes, until they are crispy and have medium brown patches. This takes about 15 minutes, or a little longer if your beans were not perfectly dry going into the pan.

2. Add some salt and a few grinds of pepper to taste. (Some brands of canned beans are prepared with salt and will need only a few sprinkles, while others will need more.) Squeeze the juice from the lemon wedge overtop and give the pan a toss. Allow the crisped beans to cool before packing. The beans will crisp up even more as they cool down to room temperature.

PACKING TIP: Pack these beans as a snack on their own, or as a part of snackbox of vegetables and crackers. They're also great sprinkled on top of a salad, like the Kale Ribbon Salad (page 113).

SMOKY BLACK BEAN DIP

MAKES: 1 CUP **ACTIVE TIME:** 5 MINS **TOTAL TIME:** 5 MINS

This smoky and zippy black bean dip is perfect for snacking on with some tortilla chips or jicama sticks, or dolloped on top of a bowl of rice, chicken, and vegetables. The smoky flavor comes from a combination of cumin and sweet smoked paprika. Sweet smoked paprika, also known as pimentón, originates from Spain; the peppers are smoked before drying, which imparts the most wonderful flavor to anything you add the paprika to. Look for a bottle or small can labeled "dolce," which means sweet or mild, rather than "picante," which can be quite spicy.

GET AHEAD: This dip can be made ahead and stored in the fridge for up to 5 days.

1 (15 oz) can black beans, drained and rinsed

Juice of 2 small limes

½ clove garlic

½ tsp ground cumin

½ tsp sweet smoked paprika

¼ tsp salt

¼ tsp pepper

½ cup chopped fresh cilantro leaves and stems

2 to 3 Tbsp olive oil

Photo on page 177

1. Put the beans, lime juice, garlic, cumin, paprika, salt, and pepper into the bowl of a food processor fitted with the steel blade. Run the processor until the beans are mashed and the garlic disappears into the purée. Scrape down the sides with a spatula.

2. Add the cilantro to the bowl and then, with the machine running, add the olive oil 1 tablespoon at a time, until you reach a smooth consistency. You may not need all of the olive oil. Taste and adjust the seasoning if needed.

PACKING TIP: Pack this tasty dip along with some tortilla chips or Bagel Chips (page 170) and fresh crunchy vegetables for a nourishing midafternoon snack. Add a quesadilla to make it a perfect midday meal.

CANNELLINI, LEMON, & BASIL DIP

MAKES: 1 CUP   **ACTIVE TIME:** 5 MINS   **TOTAL TIME:** 5 MINS

Cannellini beans, also known as white kidney beans, have a wonderful creamy texture and are the perfect base for dips. I love this lemon and basil version smeared on baguette with a handful of baby arugula or as a flavorful condiment on a grilled vegetable sandwich.

GET AHEAD: This dip can be made ahead and stored in the fridge for up to 5 days.

I (15 oz) can cannellini beans, drained and rinsed

Juice of I small lemon

½ clove garlic

½ cup packed fresh basil leaves

3 Tbsp olive oil

¼ tsp salt

¼ tsp pepper

Photo on page 174

1. Put the beans, lemon juice, and garlic into the bowl of a food processor. Process to break up the beans and finely chop the garlic, about 30 seconds. Add the basil, oil, salt, and pepper and run the processor for another 60 to 90 seconds, until the dip is completely smooth. Taste and adjust the seasoning if needed.

PACKING TIP: Pack in a container with some crostini for a satiating snack on the go, or use as part of an antipasto-inspired lunchbox.

HUMMUS

MAKES: 1 CUP   **ACTIVE TIME:** 10 MINS   **TOTAL TIME:** 10 MINS

I always have a container of hummus in my fridge—sometimes homemade and sometimes store-bought—and I like to put some out on a tray on the kitchen counter with crunchy vegetables and pita for my family to graze on when we are at home. For lunchboxes, it's great for a midmorning or midafternoon snack, or you can make it the base of your full lunch by topping it with a tomato, cucumber, pepper, and radish chopped salad and packing it with pita. Ice cubes may seem an unlikely addition to hummus, but they create an airy and creamy texture. If you haven't got ice cubes on demand, cold water will do the trick.

GET AHEAD: This hummus can be made ahead and stored in the fridge for up to 5 days.

I (15 oz) can chickpeas, rinsed and drained

Juice of I lemon

I small clove garlic

¼ cup tahini

4 ice cubes or 3 Tbsp water (see Note)

2 to 3 Tbsp olive oil

½ tsp salt

Pepper

NOTE

For a bit of variation: In step I, add ½ roasted beet to make a gorgeous and earthy-flavored pink hummus, or I cup chopped herbs (any or all of parsley, cilantro, mint, or dill) for a vibrant green dip.

1. Put the chickpeas, lemon juice, garlic, and tahini into the bowl of a food processor fitted with the steel blade. Process for about 90 seconds, until the mixture is smooth.

2. Add the ice cubes and turn on the food processor. Slowly pour the olive oil in through the feed tube, 1 tablespoon at a time, until you have achieved a creamy consistency and the ice cubes have been completely integrated, about 2 minutes.

3. Add the salt and lots of pepper and pulse the blade a few times to combine. Have a taste and adjust the seasoning as needed.

PACKING TIP: When you pack this hummus, dress it up with an extra swirl of tahini, a glug of olive oil, a few chickpeas and a generous pinch of za'atar. Pack it alongside some pita or Bagel Chips (page 176), fresh veggies, and a few olives, for a quick, easy, and nourishing meal.

DEEP GREEN FALL PESTO

MAKES: ABOUT 1 CUP   **ACTIVE TIME:** 10 MINS   **TOTAL TIME:** 10 MINS

When the basil in my garden has stopped growing in the fall and my farm box is packed with gorgeous hearty greens, I change up my usual basil pesto recipe and swap in these lovely fall brassicas. This seasonal pesto is much mellower than basil pesto, but it's equally delicious and is a great way to get your greens! It works best with kale, chard, or even the greens from a bunch of beets.

GET AHEAD: This pesto can be made ahead and stored in the fridge for up to 1 week, or freezer for up to 3 months. Freeze pesto in ice cube trays so that you can pull out only as much as you need.

1 bunch kale, thick stems removed and cut into large pieces

2 cloves garlic

¼ cup olive oil

1 cup fresh grated parmesan

½ lemon

Salt and pepper

1. Fill a medium saucepan with salted water and bring to a boil. Add the kale and garlic and cook for about 2 minutes, until the remaining stems on the kale pieces have softened.

2. Scoop the kale and garlic out of the pot and put them in a blender. Reserve ½ cup of the cooking water and drain off the rest.

3. Add the olive oil to the blender and process on medium speed until you have a smooth purée. It will be a gorgeous vibrant green!

4. Add the parmesan and pulse a few times to incorporate. Squeeze in the juice from your lemon and pulse again. If your pesto is a bit thick, add a spoonful of the cooking water and pulse a few more times. Have a taste and add salt and pepper as needed.

PACKING TIP: Toss this pesto with some pasta and leftover chicken for a quick and easy lunch, or mix a big spoonful into rice for the base of a warm or cold bowl. It's also delicious spread or spooned on top of a flatbread (see pages 71 and 75).

SUNDRIED TOMATO PESTO

MAKES: 1 CUP   **ACTIVE TIME:** 10 MINS   **TOTAL TIME:** 10 MINS

I started making this pesto after a similar product that I used to buy at the supermarket was discontinued and replaced with a trendier raw version. The new version was tasty enough but not nearly as good as the original, so I set to making it at home and was delighted to discover how quickly and easily it came together. This pesto is incredibly versatile—delicious spread on a sandwich (like the Asparagus Frittata on Brioche on page 47) or flatbread, tossed with pasta, or dolloped onto a bowl of minestrone—and comes together in under 10 minutes with pantry ingredients and some garlic.

GET AHEAD: This pesto can be made ahead and stored in the fridge for up to 1 week, or freezer for up to 3 months. Freeze in ice cube trays for convenient pre-portioned servings, it's also great on a quick bowl of pasta on a busy night.

1 cup oil-packed sundried tomatoes (about 1 (10 oz) jar), drained of most of the oil

1 small clove garlic

1 tsp red wine vinegar

Pinch chili flakes

Salt, to taste

NOTE

Grated parmesan and/or pitted black olives can add a big punch of extra flavor. Add them to the food processor with all the other ingredients and process as instructed.

1. Put the sundried tomatoes, garlic, vinegar, and chili flakes into the bowl of a food processor. Process until smooth and blended—about 1 minute. Sundried tomatoes can be salty, so taste the pesto and season with salt only if needed. Transfer to a glass jar.

PACKING TIP: Use this pesto as the sauce for an easy and flavor-packed pizza: spread it on focaccia or pita, top with shredded mozzarella, and pop into the toaster oven or under the broiler to melt. Pack with a little green salad.

FIG & BALSAMIC ONION JAM

MAKES: 1 CUP **ACTIVE TIME:** 10 MINS **TOTAL TIME:** 30 MINS

Juicy ripe figs are a magical sandwich or salad addition, but unless you live in a warm and sunny place, they can be hard to track down and extravagantly priced. I never turn down a basket of fresh figs when they are in season (and I drive home with them strapped in with the passenger-side seatbelt), but I count on dry figs for most of the year. This fig and balsamic onion jam is a great condiment spread on a sandwich, baked into a pie, or served up on a cheese board, and it impressively comes together in less than 30 minutes with ordinary pantry ingredients.

GET AHEAD: This jam can be made ahead and stored in a tightly sealed airtight container in the fridge for up to 1 week.

2 Tbsp olive oil

1 small onion, diced

½ tsp salt

Pepper

4 Tbsp balsamic vinegar

1 cup dried figs (see Note), stemmed and halved

½ cup water

NOTE

Use 1 cup roughly diced shallots in place of the onions in this recipe for a slightly milder onion flavor.

Any variety of dried fig will do the trick, but if you've recently won the lottery and can get your hands on some dried mission figs, use them to create the best version of this jam.

1. In a medium saucepan over medium heat, heat the olive oil. When the oil begins to shimmer, add the onions, salt, and a few grinds of pepper. Cook, stirring occasionally, until the onions begin to brown at the corners—about 10 minutes. Add the balsamic vinegar and cook, stirring, for 1 minute to reduce slightly. Set aside to cool down.

2. While the onions cool, put the figs and water in a small saucepan over medium-low heat. Bring to a simmer and allow to cook, partially covered with a lid, for about 15 minutes, until most of the liquid has been absorbed.

3. Transfer the onion and balsamic mixture and the figs (including any liquid in the pan) to a blender or food processor and process until smooth—about 1 minute. Taste and add salt and pepper as needed. Allow to cool, then transfer to a tightly sealed airtight container.

PACKING TIP: This jam is used in the Smoked Cheddar, Apple, & Spinach Panini (page 55) and the Grape, Feta, Kale & Rosemary Flatbread (page 68). Pack beyond this book, by throwing together a lunchbox-size cheese board: 2 or 3 wedges of different cheeses, crackers, thinly sliced apple or pear, and olives, with a little container of this delicious spread, makes for a fancy looking (but, super simple) meal.

MAPLE, ONION, & THYME JAM

MAKES: 1 CUP   **ACTIVE TIME:** 10 MINS   **TOTAL TIME:** 30 MINS

There was a restaurant in Toronto that used to have the most amazing French onion soup on the menu—the perfect antidote to our chilly winter weather. The chef shared the elaborate recipe in the newspaper several years ago and revealed that one of the things that contributed to the intense onion flavor was the way he sliced the onions. I was dubious, but I followed the recipe and, lo and behold, the onion soup was much more oniony and the onions floating in the soup were very delicate. Taking the lead from that recipe, the onions in this maple, onion, and thyme jam are sliced in the same fashion and result in a lovely jammy texture. Use this jam on sandwiches, atop grilled chicken or salmon, or on a charcuterie board; it is a great accompaniment to many cured meats and cheeses, and is a staple in our fridge.

GET AHEAD: This jam can be made ahead and stored in the fridge for up to 5 days.

2 medium yellow or red
   onions

2 Tbsp butter

2 Tbsp fresh lemon thyme
   leaves (regular thyme is a
   good substitute if you
   cannot find lemon thyme)

2 Tbsp maple syrup

Salt and pepper

2 Tbsp red wine vinegar

PACKING TIP: This jam tops the Potato, Cheddar, & Bacon Flatbread (page 76), and is spread on the Gruyère & Pear Sandwich, (page 56). It could also turn an ordinary turkey sandwich into something extraordinary, and make a salad bowl sing, with one scoop on top.

1. Peel the onions, cut off the root end and and slice in half from root to tip. Place a cut side down on your cutting board and slice along the ridges on the outside of the onion so that you are left with julienned onion rather than rainbow-like slices. Continue with the three other halves.

2. In a nonstick pan over medium heat, melt the butter. When it has melted, add the onions and cook, stirring occasionally, until the onions are translucent and starting to take on a golden color overall with some caramel-colored edges on some pieces—about 7 to 8 minutes.

3. Add the thyme, maple syrup, a big pinch of salt, and a few grinds of pepper. Continue to stir and cook until the onions have softened completely—about 10 to 12 minutes. Still stirring, add the red wine vinegar and allow most of the liquid to cook off—about 1 minute. Remove from heat and allow the onions to cool down. Taste and season with salt and pepper if needed. Transfer the jam to a tightly sealed airtight container.

ROASTED RED PEPPER SPREAD

MAKES: ABOUT ⅔ CUP   **ACTIVE TIME:** 10 MINS   **TOTAL TIME:** 30 MINS

I love to dip crunchy vegetables and pita into this smoky, tangy, and slightly sweet spread, scoop it onto grain bowls, or spread it on a sandwich. Caraway seeds have a citrus and licorice flavor and should be available with the other spices at the supermarket. Urfa pepper is a dark burgundy pepper with a smoky and mild flavor. It is a wonderful spice to have in your pantry to sprinkle on eggs or meat, but it may be harder to find at the supermarket—I have found it at large Asian and Middle Eastern shops—so you can add a pinch of chili pepper or sweet smoked paprika in its place.

GET AHEAD: This spread can be made ahead and stored in the fridge for up to I week, or freezer for up to 3 months. Use jarred roasted peppers to save time (see Note).

2 Tbsp raisins

2 Tbsp white wine vinegar

2 Tbsp olive oil

I Tbsp thinly sliced garlic (about 2 large cloves)

½ tsp ground cumin

I tsp caraway seeds

I tsp Urfa pepper

3 roasted red peppers, cut into strips (about I cup) (see Note)

Salt and pepper

NOTE

You can roast the peppers yourself, or buy them jarred to save time. Some jarred roasted red peppers are pre-salted and -spiced, so hold off on adding salt and pepper until the very end of the recipe in case the spread is already well seasoned.

1. Put the raisins and white wine vinegar in a small bowl, cover with plastic wrap, and microwave on high for 30 seconds. Set aside to cool.

2. In a medium skillet over medium heat, warm the oil. Add the garlic, cumin, caraway seeds, and Urfa pepper and cook for 2 to 3 minutes, until the garlic is golden and the kitchen is fragrant with spices.

3. Add the peppers and raisins in vinegar and cook, giving the pan an occasional shake, until the liquid has evaporated, about 5 minutes.

4. Tip the mixture into a blender and process until completely smooth. Pour the purée back into the pan and simmer over medium heat until reduced by about one-third and darkened in color. Remove from heat and allow to cool slightly. Taste and season with salt and pepper as needed.

PACKING TIP: This spread is slathered on the Grilled Broccoli, Mozzarella, & Roasted Red Pepper on Foccacia (page 5I), and is also delicious as a dip for vegetables and crackers. You could also opt not to reduce the mixture in step 4 and use it as a dressing instead, perfect for hearty greens or over roasted fall vegetables.

BAKED SWEETS & TREATS

PUMPKIN PUMPKIN SEED MINI LOAVES

MAKES: 8 MINI LOAVES   **ACTIVE TIME:** 10 MINS   **TOTAL TIME:** 35 MINS

True confession: I stayed away from all things with "pumpkin spice" for years, disgusted at the thought of something wonderful like a cappuccino ruined with pumpkin purée. Once I learned that it was just a blend of spices that I used all the time and nothing to do with an actual pumpkin, I was on board, but maybe not with the cappuccino yet. These mini loaves use both pumpkin purée and pumpkin spice as well as a generous scoop of pumpkin seeds. Pumpkin purée, not pie filling, is available in the baking aisle, but you can substitute any puréed squash, even your own roasted and puréed squash. Pumpkin spice blends are located with the rest of the spices at the supermarket.

GET AHEAD: These muffins can be made ahead and stored at room temperature for a few days, or in the freezer for up to 6 months.

2 cups all-purpose flour

2 tsp pumpkin spice

1½ tsp baking powder

½ tsp baking soda

½ tsp salt

1¼ cups pumpkin purée

2 eggs

½ cup melted butter, cooled

¼ cup milk

3 Tbsp molasses

2 Tbsp honey

2 tsp vanilla

½ cup granulated sugar

½ cup pumpkin seeds plus
    more for sprinkling

NOTE

If you haven't got an 8-cavity mini loaf pan, use a regular muffin pan to make 12 muffins instead, and reduce the baking time by about 3 minutes.

1. Preheat the oven to 350°F. Prepare an 8-cavity mini loaf pan by lining it with parchment paper liners or greasing the cups.

2. In a large bowl, whisk together the dry ingredients—flour, pumpkin spice, baking powder, baking soda, and salt.

3. In a medium bowl, whisk together the wet ingredients—pumpkin purée, eggs, butter, milk, molasses, honey, and vanilla—and the sugar until combined.

4. Pour the wet ingredients into the large bowl and mix with a rubber spatula until you cannot see any flour. Stir in the pumpkin seeds until evenly distributed.

5. Using an ice-cream scoop or large spoon, scoop the batter into the prepared loaf pan and sprinkle with more pumpkin seeds. Bake for about 25 minutes, until the tops are dark brown and a sharp knife inserted into the middle of the largest loaf comes out clean. Allow to cool in the pan for 10 minutes, then transfer a cooling rack to cool completely.

PACKING TIP: These mini loaves are a delicious treat on their own but can also be a building block for a quick and easy lunch. Pack one loaf with a couple of wedges of cheese, and some fruit and vegetables.

APPLE CARROT MUFFINS

MAKES: 12 MUFFINS　　**ACTIVE TIME:** 15 MINS　　**TOTAL TIME:** 45 MINS

These apple carrot muffins were a happy accident one morning when I set out to make a batch of morning glory muffins and realized that I didn't have a number of the ingredients on hand but had already grated the apple and carrots and preheated the oven. The golden raisins melt into the batter as they bake and leave behind sweet, caramelly pockets, and the apple, carrots, and spices come together into something reminiscent of a more virtuous carrot cake.

GET AHEAD: These muffins can be made ahead and stored at room temperature for a few days, or in the freezer for up to 6 months.

I cup all-purpose flour

I cup whole wheat flour

2 tsp baking soda

I tsp ground ginger

¼ tsp ground cloves

½ tsp salt

3 eggs, lightly beaten

¾ cup grapeseed or other neutral oil

Zest of I orange

½ cup orange juice

¾ cup packed brown sugar

1½ cups coarsely grated apples (skins on or off)

1½ cups peeled and coarsely grated carrots

¾ cup golden raisins

1. Preheat the oven to 350°F. Grease a 12-cup muffin pan or line it with paper muffin cups.

2. In a large bowl, whisk together the dry ingredients—flours, baking soda, ginger, cloves, and salt. You will know that the ingredients are evenly incorporated when you see the cloves and ginger distributed throughout the flour.

3. In a medium bowl, whisk together the wet ingredients—eggs, oil, orange zest, and orange juice—with the brown sugar until the eggs have broken up. Add the grated apples and carrots and mix in with a rubber spatula until they are evenly distributed.

4. Pour the wet ingredient mixture into the dry ingredients and mix with a rubber spatula until you cannot see any flour. Add the raisins and give the batter a few more stirs to mix them in.

5. Using an ice-cream scoop or large spoon, scoop the batter into the prepared muffin pan. Bake for about 30 minutes, or until the tops are golden brown and a sharp knife inserted into the middle of the largest muffin comes out clean. Allow to cool in the pan for 10 minutes, then transfer a cooling rack to cool completely.

PACKING TIP: Pack one of these fruit-and-vegetable-packed muffins along with a pot of yogurt for a satisfying snack.

APRICOT VANILLA MUFFINS

MAKES: 12 MUFFINS   **ACTIVE TIME:** 15 MINS   **TOTAL TIME:** 40 MINS

A perfectly sweet and ripe apricot is a rare and wonderful thing. These apricots seem to be available for just a few weeks each summer, so I satisfy my apricot cravings through the rest of the year with dried apricots eaten out of hand or baked into muffins just like these ones. Dried apricots are available in sulfured and unsulfured varieties. The sulfured variety are a brilliant, bright orange, while the unsulfured ones are a much more natural brown. They taste equally good and either one will work in this recipe.

GET AHEAD: These muffins can be made ahead and stored at room temperature for up to 3 days, or in the freezer for up to 6 months.

2 cups all-purpose flour

2 tsp baking powder

½ tsp baking soda

½ tsp salt

I cup vanilla Greek yogurt

2 eggs

I Tbsp vanilla

⅓ cup melted butter, cooled

½ cup granulated sugar

1½ cups quartered dried apricots, soaked in warm water for 10 minutes to soften and rehydrate

1. Preheat the oven to 350°F. Grease a 12-cup muffin pan or line it with paper muffin cups.

2. In a large bowl, whisk together the dry ingredients—flour, baking powder, baking soda, and salt.

3. In a medium bowl, whisk together the wet ingredients—yogurt, eggs, vanilla, and butter—and the sugar.

4. Pour the wet ingredients into the large bowl and mix with a rubber spatula until you cannot see any flour. This is a very thick batter reminiscent of cookie batter, but it will bake up to be light and fluffy. Add the drained apricots and give the batter a few more stirs to mix them in.

5. Using an ice-cream scoop or large spoon, scoop the batter into the prepared muffin pan. Bake for about 25 minutes, or until the tops are golden brown and a sharp knife inserted into the middle of the largest muffin comes out clean. Allow to cool in the pan for 10 minutes, then transfer a cooling rack to cool completely.

PACKING TIP: Pack one of these muffins alongside some fresh fruit for a perfect little afternoon snack.

CRANBERRY ORANGE MUFFINS

MAKES: 12 MUFFINS   **ACTIVE TIME:** 15 MINS   **TOTAL TIME:** 50 MINS

These muffins are an updated version of one of my favorites since childhood. My mum baked them for my brother, sister, and me when we were growing up and used to send care packages of these muffins to me and my roommate while I was away at university. I suspect that the recipe originated from a recipe booklet at the supermarket, but being a recipe of its time, it was low fat and, to compensate, very, very sweet! I have changed the recipe around to appeal to modern palates: less sugar, more berries, and a more pronounced orange flavor.

GET AHEAD: These muffins can be made ahead and stored at room temperature for up to 4 days, or in the freezer for up to 3 months.

2 cups all-purpose flour

⅔ cup granulated sugar

I tsp baking powder

½ tsp baking soda

½ tsp salt

I cup fresh or frozen cranberries

I egg

I cup orange juice

⅓ cup grapeseed or other neutral oil

I Tbsp grated orange zest

Coarse or pearl sugar, for sprinkling

1. Preheat the oven to 400°F. Grease a 12-cup muffin pan or line it with paper muffin cups.

2. In a large bowl, whisk together the dry ingredients—flour, sugar, baking powder, baking soda, and salt. Add the cranberries and mix in with a rubber spatula until they are evenly distributed.

3. In a medium bowl, whisk together the wet ingredients—eggs, orange juice, oil, and orange zest.

4. Pour the wet ingredient mixture into the dry ingredients and mix with a rubber spatula until you cannot see any flour.

5. Using an ice-cream scoop or large spoon, scoop the batter into the prepared muffin pan. Sprinkle with coarse sugar. Bake for 20 to 25 minutes, or until golden brown and a sharp knife inserted into the middle of the biggest muffin comes out clean. Allow to cool in the pan for 10 minutes, then transfer a cooling rack to cool completely. Once cool, enjoy one and pack the rest!

PACKING TIP: The tart and sweet flavor profile of these muffins pairs well with a sharp cheddar cheese for a satisfying snack that's sure to keep you going through the afternoon.

RICE PUDDING MUFFINS

MAKES: 12 MUFFINS **ACTIVE TIME:** 15 MINS **TOTAL TIME:** 1 HR 10 MINS

Whenever my kids were feeling under the weather, my mum would turn up at the door with a pan of rice pudding to comfort and heal them. These rice pudding muffins have the same vanilla and cinnamon notes and feel like a warm hug when you snack on one midmorning or to tide yourself over until dinner.

GET AHEAD: These muffins can be made ahead and stored at room temperature for up to 3 days, or in the freezer for up to 6 months.

1 cup arborio or other short-grain rice

1½ cups water

1 cinnamon stick

Salt

1½ cups all-purpose flour

1½ tsp baking powder

½ tsp baking soda

1 tsp ground cinnamon

½ cup melted butter, cooled

½ cup milk

2 eggs, lightly beaten

1 Tbsp vanilla

¾ cup granulated sugar

1. Place the rice in a sieve and rinse it under cold water until the water runs clear. Pour the rice into a medium saucepan and add the water, cinnamon stick, and a pinch of salt. Cover the pot and bring to a boil, then reduce heat to a simmer and cook for 20 minutes. Remove from heat and allow to sit for about 10 minutes with the lid on.

2. Preheat the oven to 350°F. Grease a 12-cup muffin pan or line it with paper muffin cups.

3. In a large bowl, whisk together the dry ingredients—flour, baking powder, baking soda, cinnamon, and ½ teaspoon salt.

4. In a medium bowl, whisk together the wet ingredients—butter, milk, eggs, vanilla—and the sugar.

5. Pour the wet ingredients into the large bowl and mix with a rubber spatula to combine. Remove the cinnamon stick from the rice, add the rice to the bowl and mix to combine.

6. Using an ice-cream scoop or large spoon, scoop the batter into the prepared muffin pan. Bake for about 25 minutes, or until the tops are golden brown and a sharp knife inserted into the middle of the largest muffin comes out clean. Allow to cool in the pan before transferring to a cooling rack to cool completely.

PACKING TIP: Pack with some fresh berries for a perfect midmorning or midafternoon snack.

CINNAMON SUGAR YOGURT BITES

MAKES: 10 YOGURT BITES   **ACTIVE TIME:** 15 MINS   **TOTAL TIME:** 30 MINS

These yogurt bites are impossibly easy to make and a greater-than-the-sum-of-the-ingredients treat. They are perfect as a little snack with some fruit or as a sweet treat at lunchtime. I keep a stash of these in my freezer and pop them frozen into our lunchboxes—they always defrost in time for lunch hour.

GET AHEAD: These bites can be made ahead and stored at room temperature for 2 to 3 days, or in the freezer for up to 3 months.

¾ cup all-purpose flour

1¼ tsp baking powder

½ tsp salt

½ cup vanilla yogurt

I egg, lightly beaten

2 Tbsp granulated sugar

2 tsp ground cinnamon

1. Preheat the oven to 350°F and line a baking sheet with parchment paper.

2. In a bowl, whisk together the flour, baking powder, and salt. Add the yogurt and, using a rubber spatula, mix to form a dough. You may find it easier to use your hands toward the end to combine the last bits of flour.

3. Transfer the dough to a lightly floured surface and knead until smooth. Add a bit of flour if your dough is sticky.

4. Cut the dough into 10 equal pieces and roll into balls. This is a rustic snack so perfection is not important, but aim for a shape that is uniform in size so that they will bake evenly.

5. Place the egg in a small bowl. In a separate small bowl, combine the sugar and cinnamon.

6. Dip each dough ball into the beaten egg and then roll it in the sugar mixture. Place on the prepared baking sheet and repeat until you have dipped and rolled each ball.

7. Bake for about 15 minutes, until medium brown and crispy on the outside. Enjoy warm or at room temperature.

PACKING TIP: These sweet bites are surprisingly satisfying thanks to the yogurt. Pack them along with some fresh fruit for a sweet snack.

BANANA CHOCOLATE CHIP SOFT COOKIES

MAKES: 12 SOFT COOKIES   **ACTIVE TIME:** 15 MINS   **TOTAL TIME:** 45 MINS

These "soft cookies" are what I used to call muffin tops, when muffin tops were the delicious domed lid of a muffin with satisfying crispy edges and not the result of pants that are too tight or cut too low! The recipe is based on an old one that I recorded in a little spiral-bound book when I was in university, and it's one of those basic, reliable recipes—not fancy, just perfectly simple. My kids adore them, and I make them whenever the bananas that sit in a bowl on our counter have gone from perfect for eating to just a bit too soft and speckled to be enjoyed out of hand. If you haven't got a muffin top pan, you can use a regular muffin pan and extend the baking time by 10 minutes.

GET AHEAD: These soft cookies can be made ahead and stored at room temperature for up to 3 days, or in the freezer for up to 6 months.

1 cup all-purpose flour

½ cup granulated sugar

1½ tsp baking powder

¼ tsp salt

3 bananas, mashed

1 egg

½ cup melted butter, cooled

½ cup vanilla yogurt

¾ cup chocolate chips (dark and caramelized white chocolate are our favorites) plus extra for topping (optional)

NOTE

If you don't have two muffin top pans (and who does?), bake these cookies in two batches. Just allow the pan to cool and then spray or butter it again between uses.

1. Preheat the oven to 350°F. Prepare 2 six-cavity muffin top pans by spraying them with baking spray or buttering them (see Note).

2. In a large bowl, whisk together the dry ingredients—flour, sugar, baking powder, and salt.

3. In a medium bowl, whisk together the wet ingredients—bananas, egg, butter, and yogurt.

4. Pour the wet ingredients into the large bowl and mix with a rubber spatula until you cannot see any flour. Fold in the chocolate chips and stir until they are evenly distributed.

5. Using an ice-cream scoop or large spoon, scoop the batter into the prepared muffin top pans. Gently press a few extra chocolate chips on top of each cookie if you'd like. Bake for about 15 minutes, until the tops are golden brown with dark edges and a sharp knife inserted into the middle of the largest cookie comes out clean. Allow to cool in the pan before transferring to a cooling rack to cool completely.

PACKING TIP: Pack one of these soft cookies with an assortment of fruit for the perfect sweet snack.

BAKED PEAR, VANILLA, & SPICE DONUTS

MAKES: 12 (4-INCH) DONUTS   **ACTIVE TIME:** 15 MINS   **TOTAL TIME:** 40 MINS

If you ever find yourself, as I often do every autumn, with an abundance of ripe, juicy pears, these baked donuts are for you! The sweet pear and gentle, warming spices taste delicious alongside a cup of tea mid-morning or as a sweet treat in your lunchbox. I use either Anjou or Bartlett pears but substitute with whatever you have on hand.

GET AHEAD: These donuts can be made ahead and stored at room temperature for up to 4 days, or in the freezer for up to 3 months.

4 pears, peeled, cored and roughly chopped (see Note)

¼ tsp ground ginger

½ tsp cinnamon

I tsp vanilla extract

½ cup buttermilk

I egg

I Tbsp vanilla

½ cup packed light brown sugar

2 cups all-purpose flour

I tsp ground ginger

¼ tsp ground nutmeg

½ tsp salt

I½ tsp baking powder

½ cup melted butter, cooled

Icing sugar, for dusting

NOTE

Store leftover sauce in the fridge for up to 5 days and use as you would apple sauce. No time to make pear sauce? Substitute puréed pear from the baby-food aisle.

1. Place the pears, ginger, cinnamon and vanilla in a saucepan over medium heat. Cover and cook, stirring occasionally, until the pears are soft. Remove the lid and continue to cook until most of the liquid has evaporated. Allow to cool. When cool, mash with a fork or masher to create a smooth sauce.

2. Preheat the oven to 350°F. Prepare your donut pan by spraying it with cooking spray.

3. In a large bowl, combine 1 cup of the pear sauce, with the buttermilk, egg, vanilla, and brown sugar and stir with a rubber spatula until the mixture is uniform. Add the flour, ginger, nutmeg, salt, and baking powder and stir until well combined.

4. Pour the melted butter into the bowl and carefully fold it into the rest of the batter. It takes about a minute to integrate the butter, but it will mix in!

5. Fill a piping bag with the donut batter and pipe it into the prepared pan. Fill each section about halfway. If you don't have a piping bag, you can also spoon the batter into the pan. Bake the donuts for 12 to 15 minutes, or until firm to the touch and a sharp knife inserted into one comes out clean. Allow to cool in the pan for 10 minutes, then flip out onto a cooling rack and dust with icing sugar. Once cool, enjoy one and pack the rest.

PACKING TIP: Tuck one of these indulgent donuts into your lunchbox for a sweet treat, or pack one with some sliced fruit (try apples and pears) for a tasty afternoon treat.

BAKED CHOCOLATE BANANA DONUTS

MAKES: 12 (4-INCH) DONUTS   **ACTIVE TIME:** 15 MINS   **TOTAL TIME:** 40 MINS

I picked up a donut pan to make donuts for Hanukkah one year, and it wasn't until I was decluttering my kitchen about a year ago that it occurred to me that I could use it year-round! These chocolate banana donuts are cakey, chocolaty, and delicious. Thanks to the pan, they are just as easy to throw together as a batch of muffins and are an indulgent way to use up ripe bananas.

GET AHEAD: These donuts can be made ahead and stored at room temperature for up to 4 days, or in the freezer for up to 3 months.

2 bananas, mashed

½ cup buttermilk

1 egg

1 tsp vanilla

½ cup packed light brown sugar

½ cup cocoa powder (extra dark if you can find it)

1½ cups all-purpose flour

2 tsp ground cinnamon

1½ tsp baking powder

½ tsp salt

½ cup melted butter, cooled

Photo on page 70

1. Preheat the oven to 350°F. Prepare your donut pan by spraying it with cooking spray.

2. In a large bowl, combine the bananas, buttermilk, egg, vanilla, and brown sugar and stir with a rubber spatula until the mixture is uniform.

3. Add the cocoa powder, flour, cinnamon, baking powder, and salt and stir until well combined.

4. Pour the melted butter into the bowl and carefully fold it into the mixture. It takes about a minute to integrate the butter, but it will mix in! You will have a relatively thick, chocolatey batter when everything has been combined.

5. Fill a piping bag with the donut batter and pipe it into the prepared pan. Fill each section about halfway. If you don't have a piping bag, you can also spoon the batter into the pan. Bake for 12 to 15 minutes, until the donuts are firm to the touch and a sharp knife inserted into one comes out clean.

6. Allow to cool in the pan for 10 minutes, then flip them out onto a cooling rack to cool completely. Once cool, enjoy one and store the rest.

PACKING TIP: Tuck one of these donuts into a lunchbox for a sweet treat (see the photo on page 70), or packed alongside some berries for a little afternoon pick-me-up.

MAPLE SEED BRITTLE

MAKES: ⅓ CUP   **ACTIVE TIME:** 5 MINS   **TOTAL TIME:** 5 MINS

Seed brittle does double duty as a sweet, crunchy treat or a fun addition to a hearty salad. This recipe has only two ingredients and doesn't require any special candy-making skills—just a pan, some seeds, and some maple syrup. And you can easily multiply this recipe to make a much bigger batch if you like.

GET AHEAD: This brittle can be made ahead and stored at room temperature for up to 1 month.

⅓ cup pumpkin seeds

2 Tbsp maple syrup

NOTE

Add a pinch of cayenne pepper to the seed brittle to create a sweet and spicy treat!

Photo on page 38

1. Line a baking sheet with parchment paper and set aside.

2. Warm a small nonstick skillet over medium heat. Add the pumpkin seeds and maple syrup and stir to combine. Allow the mixture to come to a very, very gentle boil, giving the pan a shake every so often, and cook for 4 to 5 minutes, until the syrup has caramelized around the seeds and the seeds are glossy and coated. If you remove a seed and some syrup from the pan with a spatula, the syrup should harden like a hard caramel almost immediately.

3. Remove from heat and pour out onto the baking sheet, using an offset or rubber heatproof spatula to spread the seeds into a single layer. Allow to cool. When cool, break into pieces.

PACKING TIP: Pack a little container of these seeds with your lunch for a lovely sweet treat, or pack with some yogurt and fruit for a more satisfying midmorning or midafternoon snack.

GRANOLA BARS

MAKES: 8 BARS OR 16 SQUARES **ACTIVE TIME:** 5 MINS **TOTAL TIME:** 35 MINS

Granola bars, like granola, are simple and inexpensive to make and are easily customizable. The base of this recipe is oats, oil, and a sweetening agent like honey or maple syrup, and the rest is up to you! I usually buy dried fruits and seeds in bulk, and because the selection varies seasonally, I use whatever I have on hand. This means that we have dried cherry, sunflower seed, and mini dark chocolate chip granola bars in the fall, and raisin, cranberry, flax, and pumpkin seed bars in the spring. No matter what time of year, I normally set out my I cup measure after I have measured out the oats and add handfuls of mix-ins until the cup is full, then add them to the mixing bowl.

GET AHEAD: These granola bars can be made ahead and stored at room temperature for at least I week, or in the freezer for up to 3 months.

1¾ cups rolled oats

I cup total mix-ins of your choice (sunflower seeds, pumpkin seeds, flax seeds, raisins, dried cranberries, mini chocolate chips, etc.)

½ cup grapeseed or sunflower oil

½ cup honey, maple syrup, or other liquid sweetener

1. Preheat the oven to 325°F and line an 8-inch square baking pan with parchment paper.

2. In a medium mixing bowl, place all the ingredients and stir to combine. Tip the mixture into the prepared pan and use a spatula to spread it out evenly. With wet hands, pack the mixture down firmly.

3. Bake for 25 to 30 minutes, or until the top is golden brown. While still warm and soft, use a sharp knife or the edge of a bench scraper to divide the pan into bars (or squares, if you prefer). Allow the bars to cool to room temperature and crisp up before removing them from the pan.

PACKING TIP: Tuck one of these granola bars into a lunchbox for a sweet lunchtime treat, or pack one on its own with some grapes or other sweet and juicy fruit and a container of yogurt for a midmorning or midafternoon snack.

SWEET HANDPIES

MAKES: 6 SMALL HANDPIES   **ACTIVE TIME:** 10 MINS   **TOTAL TIME:** 25 MINS

These small handpies are the perfect little indulgence after lunch or with a cup of coffee or tea. Thanks to frozen puff pastry, they take only a few minutes to put together and are incredibly versatile. There are three sweet filling options here, but play around with what you have on hand.

GET AHEAD: These handpies can be prepared ahead of time; see page 149 for your options.

HANDPIES

1 sheet puff pastry, thawed but cold

1 egg, lightly beaten

1 Tbsp granulated sugar

BANANA CARAMEL FILLING

1 cup mashed ripe banana (about 1 large banana)

¾ cup caramel chips (white chocolate chips work well too)

RICOTTA BLUEBERRY FILLING

¾ cup whole-milk ricotta

6 Tbsp blueberry jam

Zest of 1 orange

APPLE, HONEY, & CINNAMON FILLING

2 apples, peeled and thinly sliced

1 Tbsp honey

1 tsp ground cinnamon

1. Preheat the oven to 400°F and line a baking sheet with parchment paper. On a lightly floured surface, unroll the puff pastry sheet. Using a sharp knife or pastry cutter, cut it into three 4 × 12-inch rectangles. Cut each of these rectangles horizontally into four, so that you end up with twelve 3 × 4-inch rectangles. Six rectangles will be the bottoms of your handpies, and the other six will serve as the tops. Alternatively, use a 2-inch cookie cutter to cut your sheet of puff pastry into 16 circles to make 8 little circular pies.

2. Mix or toss your chosen filling ingredients together in a bowl. Transfer the six bottom rectangles (or 8 circles) to the baking sheet to fill them, dividing the filling carefully between them, and leaving a ¼-inch border around all edges (see Note). Using a pastry brush, paint the ¼-inch border of the bottom rectangles (or circles) with a little of the beaten egg.

3. Using the point of a sharp knife, cut a small vent in each of the top rectangles (or circles) to allow steam to escape while baking. Carefully top each filled bottom rectangle (or circle) with a top "lid." Use your fingers or a fork to gently press down and seal all the edges. Brush the tops generously with the remaining beaten egg and sprinkle with sugar. Bake for 15 minutes, until puffed up and golden brown (the pies will be crispy, and you'll see that the lovely layers of pastry have puffed up along the edges).

PACKING TIP: Allow the pies to cool completely before packing. If they're still warm, pack them in a paper or fabric sandwich bag to preserve the crispy pastry.

NOTE

Resist the urge to overfill the pies—they will invariably explode in the oven and leave you with a half-empty pie!

RECIPES BY CATEGORY

GREAT FOR KIDS

Bacon & Egg Handpies 26
Egg, Greens, & Cheese Tortilla 30
Infallible Crepes 39
Pumpkin Spice Waffles 35
Lemon Ricotta Pancakes 40
Basic Crunchy Granola 43
Smoked Cheddar, Apple, & Spinach
    Panini 55
Gruyère & Pear Sandwich 56
Curried Chicken Salad Sandwich 65
Potato, Cheddar, & Bacon Flatbread 76
Parmesan Broth with Vegetables &
    Tortellini 89
Chicken Soup 95
Carrot, Currant, & Mint Salad 109
Cucumber, Dill, & Yogurt Salad 110
Spinach, Orange, & Chicken Salad 125
Fresh Roll Bowl 131
Southwestern Bowl 132
Sesame Noodles 135
Sushi Bowl 136
Crispy Tofu or Chicken Bowl 139
French Onion Soup Pasta 164
Chicken Pot Pie Stew 168
Quick Spaghetti Bolognese 171
Puff Pastry Cheese Sticks 175
Bagel Chips 176
Crispy Cannellini Beans 179

HEALTHY SNACKS

Crispy Cannellini Beans 179
Smoky Black Bean Dip 180
Cannellini, Lemon, and Basil Dip 181
Hummus 183
Pumpkin Pumpkin Seed Mini Loaves 193
Apple Carrot Muffins 194
Apricot Vanilla Muffins 195
Cranberry Orange Muffins 196
Rice Pudding Muffins 199
Cinnamon Sugar Yogurt Bites 200
Granola Bars 209

SUGGESTED LUNCH PLANS

How does the saying go? If you fail to plan, you plan to fail? The good news is that failing to plan your lunches isn't really a failure, but to get you started—or to keep you going if you are stuck in a lunch packing rut—here is a collection of lunch packing plans that deliver a real variety of flavors and types of meals over two weeks. There is a plan perfect for kids, followed by two seasonal meal plans, as well a plan that sets you up with a week of dinners and corresponding reimagined lunches for the next day. The final plan, the Make Ahead, is for the dedicated meal planner. The recipes featured here can all be made on a Sunday (or any day when you have a big block of time) and popped into the fridge or freezer for later on in the week.

Create the lunch packing roadmap that makes sense for you, your family, and your lifestyle. I promise you will thank your former self when you open the fridge to find it already stocked with everything you need to make lunch!

KID-FRIENDLY LUNCH PLAN

	MONDAY	TUESDAY	WEDNESDAY	THURSDAY	FRIDAY
WEEK 1	Bacon & Egg Handpies (page 26)	Sesame Noodles (page 135)	Chicken Soup (page 95)	Pumpkin Spice Waffles (page 35)	Exceptional Egg Salad Sandwich (page 48)
WEEK 2	Roasted Tomato Soup (page 81), with grilled cheese soldiers for dipping	Infallible Crepes (page 39) with fresh berries	Potato, Cheddar, & Bacon Flatbread (page 76)	Hummus (page 183), Bagel Chips (page 176) and veggies	Chicken Pot Pie Stew Handpie (page 168)

HOT WEATHER LUNCH PLAN

	MONDAY	TUESDAY	WEDNESDAY	THURSDAY	FRIDAY
WEEK 1	Lemon Ricotta Pancakes (page 40)	Goat Cheese, Peach, & Basil Panini (page 52)	Fresh Roll Bowl (page 131)	Summer Caprese (page 118)	Carrot, Currant, & Mint Salad (page 109) with Cucumber, Dill, & Yogurt Salad (page 110)
WEEK 2	Asparagus Frittata on Brioche (page 47)	Vibrant Quinoa Salad (page 104)	Egg, Greens, & Cheese Tortilla (page 30)	Grilled Zucchini, Preserved Lemon, & Herb Flatbread (page 72)	Curried Chicken Salad Sandwich (page 65)

COLD WEATHER LUNCH PLAN

	MONDAY	TUESDAY	WEDNESDAY	THURSDAY	FRIDAY
WEEK 1	Pumpkin Spice Waffles (page 35)	Creamy Corn & Potato Chowder (page 93)	Farro Niçoise (page 122)	French Onion Soup Pasta Handpie (page 164)	Gruyère & Pear Sandwich (page 56)
WEEK 2	Butternut Squash, Leek, Goat Cheese, & Pesto Flatbread (page 75)	Roasted Cauliflower, Manouri, & Pomegranate Salad (page 107)	Sweet Potato & Onion Frittata (page 33)	Curried Leek & Potato Soup (page 85)	Moroccan Spice Stew (page 157)

TONIGHT'S DINNER + TOMORROW'S LUNCH PLAN

	SUNDAY DINNER / MONDAY LUNCH	MONDAY DINNER / TUESDAY LUNCH	TUESDAY DINNER / WEDNESDAY LUNCH	WEDNESDAY DINNER / THURSDAY LUNCH	THURSDAY DINNER / FRIDAY LUNCH
TONIGHT'S DINNER	Quick Spaghetti Bolognese (the recipe on page 171 makes enough for 2)	Tofu Katsu (the recipe on page 61 makes enough for 2) and add rice and stir-fried vegetables	Roast chicken, roasted potatoes, and grilled corn on the cob	Farro Niçoise (the recipe on page 122 makes enough for 2)	Grilled chicken breasts or thighs, steamed asparagus, and orzo tossed with some olive oil and a squeeze of lemon juice
PREP FOR THE MORNING	Double (or more) the recipe to have enough leftover for handpies tomorrow	Double (or more) the tofu quantity to have enough leftover for sandwiches tomorrow	Make extra potatoes and corn to have enough leftover to make chowder for tomorrow; shred any leftover chicken	When hard-boiling the eggs, make 4 extra, enough for sandwiches tomorrow	Make extra asparagus and orzo to have enough leftover for bowls tomorrow; slice leftover chicken
TOMORROW'S LUNCH	Quick Spaghetti Bolognese Handpies (page 171)	Tofu Katsu Sandwich (page 61)	Creamy Corn and Potato Chowder (page 93) (with optional shredded roast chicken added)	Exceptional Egg Salad Sandwich (page 48)	Chickpea, Asparagus, and Orzo Bowl (page 128) (substituting the chickpeas for leftover chicken if preferred)

MAKE-AHEAD PLAN

	MONDAY	TUESDAY	WEDNESDAY	THURSDAY	FRIDAY
WEEK 1	Beet & Citrus Salad (page 100)	Roasted Tomato Soup (page 81)	Autumn Caprese (page 121)	Moroccan Spice Stew (page 157)	Carrot & Orange Soup (page 82)
MAKE AHEAD	Roast, peel and slice beets; prepare the dressing. Store in the fridge.	Make soup. Freeze in portions.	Roast squash; prepare the dressing. Store in the fridge.	Make stew and cook accompanying rice. Freeze separately in portions.	Make soup. Freeze in portions.
WEEK 2	Farro Niçoise (page 122)	Curried Sweet Potatoes, Chickpeas, & Spinach Bowl (page 154)	Roasted Cauliflower, Manouri, & Pomegranate Salad (page 107)	Chicken Soup (page 95)	Lemon Ricotta Pancakes (page 40)
MAKE AHEAD	Cook farro; hard boil eggs; steam beans; prepare the dressing. Store in the fridge.	Make the curry and the accompanying rice. Freeze separately in portions.	Roast cauliflower; prepare the dressing. Store in the fridge.	Make soup. Freeze in portions.	Make pancakes. Freeze in portions.

ACKNOWLEDGEMENTS

In February 2020, when Michelle Arbus reached out to me about writing a book about packed lunches, I never imagined that I would spend the next 20 months of school closures, stay-at-home restrictions, and general pandemic life barely packing any actual lunches! I also had no idea how much work and how many people are involved in creating a cookbook; I am so grateful to have had this opportunity and to work with an exceptional group at Penguin Random House Canada. Thank you, Michelle, for opening the door to the world of publishing for me.

Thank you, Robert McCullough, for your warm welcome to the Appetite family and for your immediate enthusiasm for this book. Our initial conversations set the tone for every PRHC meeting I have had since then and I have been impressed and so reassured as a cookbook writing novice to find that everyone I interact with shares the same enthusiasm and commitment to creating a high-quality end product.

Massive thanks to Lindsay Paterson for patiently guiding me through every step of this process, always quick with words of encouragement and constructive and insightful feedback. It has been an absolute delight to collaborate with you!

Thank you to Emma Dolan for the beautiful and easy-to-navigate design, as well as for taking my (non-designer) input into consideration. The end result has far exceeded my expectations.

Thank you to everyone who laid their eyes on this book during the publishing process—the proofreaders, copy editors, and interns—for your careful and detailed work that not only caught my mistakes and clumsy wording, but played a key role in the quality of the book. Thanks especially to Sam MacKinnon for your time teaching me about photography and photo editing, and to Whitney Millar for the tasks that I have always taken for granted as a book reader (but will not any longer!), and to Erin Cooper for your stellar typesetting skills and attention to detail with every line.

Finally, huge thanks to my family who, lucky for me (perhaps not always lucky for them) were my captive audience and resident tasters, testers, and critics. Evan, Noa, and Talia, you were the greatest cheerleaders and very graciously ate "something from the book" for weeks on end without complaint. Hopefully this was as big of a perk for all of you while attending virtual school and working from home as it was for me!

INDEX